WHAT OTHERS ARE SAYING

"We desperately need a generation of young people who will read *The Burn Factor* and discover the God who can do above and beyond what they dream possible. Parents, pastors, and youth leaders, please put a copy of this book in the hands of every young person in your care!"

Ron Luce, Founder and President of
Teen Mania International

"I have known Randy Lawrence for fifteen years. First as a student and then as a friend. Randy is the real deal. He will be a history maker. His new book *The Burn Factor* is certainly needed in this season where grace is sold cheap on the altar of Christian convenience. While much of today's Christian literature is little more than a Gerber's gospel, *The Burn Factor* is what Leonard Ravenhill would call "Meat for Men." Randy courageously reintroduces biblical concepts like commitment and sacrifice. This book is a "must read" for anyone who wants enough of God to make a real impact on their generation. I pray you will be spiritually blindsided by this excellent book."

Dr. Larry Martin, River of Revival Ministries
Author of multiple books and Editor of
The Complete Azusa Street Library

WHAT OTHERS ARE SAYING

"Some books aren't for you. This could be one of those books. If you are the person who doesn't want to be challenged to grow in your faith: this isn't for you. If you are the person who is nominal in your passion about Jesus: this isn't for you. If you are the person who is satisfied with status quo in your walk with God: this isn't for you. BUT—if you are the person who is crying out inside with a burning zeal to live consumed for Jesus Christ—get busy. Read every page. Read them again and again. And you will discover *The Burn Factor*."

Charles G. Scott, General Bishop PCG
and Author of
Storms Don't Bother Me

"*The Burn Factor* will awaken and stir the passion for Christ in your life. As you read Randy's personal stories and insights, you will find your heart yearning for God's "double portion" anointing for your life. This book will set you on a fresh journey of intimacy for Christ.

Richard Crisco, Senior Pastor Rochester First Assembly
and Author of
It's Time: Passing Revival to the Next Generation

WHAT OTHERS ARE SAYING

"Randy's easy-reading style of writing makes this book a pleasure to read, yet the depth of the content will challenge any person who is serious about their faith. It is obvious that what Randy has to say in *The Burn Factor* comes straight from his heart and life experience. This book will be a great benefit to today's leaders and to future generations who desire to go to the next level."

Josh Pennington, Senior Pastor Christpoint Church
Galena, Kansas

"Randy Lawrence is doing what he does best. He communicates with conviction and from experience the fight against a usual life. Randy writes in *The Burn Factor* a powerful message that most people don't grasp: the belief that God has placed something significant in all of us. This book will help you release that potential and dream God-sized dreams."

Joe Skiles, Executive Pastor Solid Rock Family Church
Jefferson City, Missouri

WHAT OTHERS ARE SAYING

"Randy is a compelling and catalytic leader. His passion for the pursuit of God burns brightly and impacts every generation. His book *The Burn Factor* is dangerous if you are looking to remain in the comfort zone of Christian faith. Through examining the biblical story of Elijah and Elisha, Randy dares every Christ-follower to approach their own "double portion" or "something more" in God. If you are sensing a need to "fan the flame of your faith," then *The Burn Factor* is for you!"

Dr. Wayman Ming Jr., President and Founder of Exceed International and Author of
Re-Forming a New You

"Getting to know Randy personally is a gift. His longing to see everyone step into their God-given call is not only relevant but crucial. We need a generation of Elijah's who will see the potential in others and a generation of Elisha's who will dare to believe God for greater things. Read this book prayerfully as it will fulfill an assignment in your life. The next chapter in God's story isn't just up to Him…it's up to you. Thank you, Randy, for being who you are and inviting us into an encounter."

Heath Adamson, National Youth Director Assemblies of God and Author of
The Bush Always Burns

THE BURN FACTOR

ALL FOR THE CALL

RANDY K. LAWRENCE

M PRINTS

Copyright © 2015 Randy Lawrence Jr.
All rights reserved.

Published by MPRINTS Publishing
PO Box 850
Joplin, Missouri 64801

This book or any portion thereof may not be reproduced or used in any manner whatsoever without the express written permission of the publisher except for the use of brief quotations in a book review.

Cover Photo Credit: Josh Rogers

Unless otherwise indicated, all Scripture quotations are taken from the Holy Bible, New King James Version. Copyright © 1982 by Thomas Nelson, Inc. Used by permission. All rights reserved.

Scripture quotations marked (NLT) are taken from the Holy Bible, New Living Translation, copyright © 1996, 2004, 2007 by Tyndale House Foundation. Used by permission of Tyndale House Publishers, Inc., Carol Stream, Illinois, 60188. All rights reserved.

Scripture quotations marked The Message are from *The Message: The Bible in Contemporary Language*. Copyright © 1999 by NavPress. Used by permission. All rights reserved.

Scripture quotations marked (AMP) are taken from the Amplified Bible. Copyright © 1954, 1958, 1962, 1964, 1965, 1987 by the Lockman Foundation. Used by permission.

Printed in the United States of America

First Printing, 2015

ISBN: 978-1-4951-3738-9

DEDICATION

To my Father and Mother, who have lived out the heart of this book every day of my life. I am who I am because of you.

CONTENTS

Foreword — 1
Introduction — 5

A DOUBLE PORTION

CHAPTER 1: *Is There Really More?* — 9
CHAPTER 2: *A Strange Request* — 15
CHAPTER 3: *Take It or Forsake It* — 23

EMBRACE THE CALL

CHAPTER 4: *Blindsided* — 33
CHAPTER 5: *Choices* — 41
CHAPTER 6: *The First Step* — 49

BURN THE BACKUP

CHAPTER 7: *No Plan B* — 59
CHAPTER 8: *Out of the Comfort Zone* — 69
CHAPTER 9: *The Burn Factor* — 77

START NOW

CHAPTER 10: *Holy Hustle* — 87
CHAPTER 11: *Serve* — 95
CHAPTER 12: *Submitted* — 105

DIVINE FOCUS

CHAPTER 13: *Straight Ahead* — 115
CHAPTER 14: *The Power of "No"* — 123
CHAPTER 15: *Hungry for More* — 133

CONCLUSION

CHAPTER 16: *Go for It* — 143
Endnotes — 147
Acknowledgements — 155
About the Author — 157

FOREWORD

YOUR PERSONAL ADVENTURE

Have you ever noticed how you're hardwired for story? We all are. Whether watching a movie, reading a book, or hearing a tale told by a campfire, we find ourselves engaged with hopes, fears, temptations, challenges, and wonderments of people in hard or humorous or crazy situations.

The Bible is full of stories, and Jesus told lots of them. We're shaped, inspired, convicted, and lifted by parables and literature and true-life tales. From Lord of the Rings and Star Wars to Anna Karenina and Tom Sawyer, we absorb insights into good and evil and the great challenges of life.

Randy tells stories. Elijah and Elisha stories. And Jesus stories. And stories out of his life that interweave with Bible truths and possibilities and promises.

I personally resonate with Randy's stories, and with his drawing guidance and inspiration from the Bible. Like him, I spent many good years in youth work and editing a magazine called Campus Life. They were years of intense prayer and marvelous moments of seeing God at work in students' lives. It was a time when I responded to Jeremiah 33:3: "Call to me, and I will answer you, and show you great and mighty things." God has been faithful over the years in doing just that.

Randy opens doors to show what happens when we respond to God's invitations. Your story is and will be different from Randy's and mine, but the biblical stories and their spiritual principles are the same. May you glean from them challenges and inspiration as you respond to God's call to adventure and discipleship.

—Harold Myra

Harold Myra was a club and rally director and editor for *Youth for Christ* and later the CEO of *Christianity Today International* for 32 years. He is the author of *The One Year Book of Encouragement*.

INTRODUCTION

"Please let a double portion of your spirit be upon me." —Elisha

July 6, 1998, is a benchmark date in my life.

With about 20 other teenagers from our youth group, I piled into our church bus and made the 700-mile-plus trip down to Pensacola, Florida, to attend "The Elisha Generation" Youth Conference. It was there in the Pensacola Civic Center, at age 15, that I had a personal encounter with God that radically changed my life.

The experience was and still is hard to describe in words.

This book, however, isn't as much about that encounter as it is about the days, months, and years that have followed.

God intervened into my "normal" Christian life and set me on a radical journey that has been nothing shy of miraculous. It is hard for me to imagine what my life would have been like without this pivotal moment.

During my spiritual awakening and in the years that followed, God used the story of Elijah and Elisha in a very significant way. For those familiar with the story, we know that Elisha inherited a double portion of the anointing that was on Elijah's life. I believe with all of my heart that God has a double portion of His anointing available for whoever is ready to step up to the plate and go all in with Him.

In this book, we will look at Elisha's encounter with God's calling on his life and how he responded to that call. I believe that as we look at the story of Elisha, we see an incredible blueprint to follow for our own lives.

On the last night of the conference, host Pastor Richard Crisco issued the following challenge:

"If you did not get what you wanted from God this week, you either didn't want it, or you tried to bargain with the price."

I left determined that week, like never before, to focus on God's plan for my life. I wasn't going to sell out or settle for anything less than that for which God had created me.

I pray that as you read over the pages that follow that God will awaken a deep hunger on the inside of you to experience a double portion of God's Spirit and anointing. I'm asking God to wreck your life in such a way that you will be completely dissatisfied with the *status quo*.

When everything is said and done, may history record of us, that just like Elisha, we possessed *The Burn Factor*.

—Randy Lawrence

SECTION 1

A DOUBLE PORTION

CHAPTER 1

IS THERE REALLY MORE?

"May the Lord give you increase more and more" —Psalm 115:14

I still remember standing on the porch of a pastor friend's house as I did something that I was all too familiar with doing, waiting for my Dad to finish his conversation. Growing up as a PK (Pastor's Kid) in a small town, I felt like my Dad had a permanent sign on his back that stated, "Available for lengthy conversations." Seriously, my parents were not only deeply loved by their congregants, community, friends, and family, but they were also always genuinely concerned for others, so lengthy conversations were nothing out of the ordinary.

But something was different about this conversation on that cool southwest Virginia evening. As I stood there waiting as I had thousands of other times, something was said that I will never forget.

It was one single sentence. One single sentence that sparked a journey that I would soon set out on that would forever change the trajectory of my life.

I was fifteen years old at the time, school was out, and like many of my other peers, I was "stoked" out of my mind to kick off summer. I must add that this jubilant mood helped me be a little extra patient that night as I waited for the conversation to end. As the conversation came to a close (causing my heart rate to beat at an accelerated pace), the pastor friend turned to me to say his goodbyes.

I could literally see the finish line for the evening, when my Father stated to him that I was getting ready to leave for a youth conference with the students in our church. And then he said it: "The conference is called "'The Elisha Generation": Receiving a Double Portion of God's Spirit!'" As he stated the "double portion of God's Spirit" line, I'll never forget the look in my Dad's face.

That was it. That was the line that changed everything for me.

As we drove home that night, I couldn't help but think about that phrase, "double portion." Having grown up in church my entire life, I was familiar with the story of Elijah and Elisha; however, it was cataloged away with all the other flannel board Sunday School character stories. For those of you who don't know what a flannel board is, you've missed out on awesomeness. Google it. And if you don't know what Sunday School is, just imagine story time (Bible stories of course), with cookies and a juice box. Oh, and yes, you get also get a sticker for coming! #nailedit

Even though I knew the story, I must confess that the whole "double portion" thing was not something I really understood. I pondered that line for a few minutes, and then it wasn't long until my mind shuffled along to the next track as we finished our trip home. But, make no mistake about it, that line was forever imprinted on both my mind, and more importantly, my heart.

A double portion? Could there really be such a thing?

THE GOD OF MORE AND MORE

Ephesians 3:20 states, "Now to Him who is able to do exceedingly abundantly above all that we ask or think." If you've grown up in church, surely you've heard this Scripture. You've probably also heard

CH1: IS THERE REALLY MORE?

this popular line, "God has more for your life!" But I wonder, do we really believe that God has more for our lives? Do we know the God of more? Do we know the God of the double portion? Or is this a part of the flannelgraph story of our faith that we have simply forgotten or have yet to discover? Little did I know that this one simple phrase, "A double portion of God's Spirit," would forever change my life and send me on the most amazing journey ever!

You see, growing up I was a drug addict. Yes, you read that right, a drug addict and one from a very young age. Daddy and Momma drug me to Sunday School, they drug me to Sunday morning worship, Sunday night service, prayer meeting, business meeting, you name it, if the church doors were open, I was there! So I was very familiar with God, I personally knew Him and was a good young "Christian" boy. However, I was experiencing just enough of God to get by.

I knew all about Him, but didn't really know Him. I had yet to experience the God of more. I had just enough faith to get me by, but not enough to really experience anything like a double portion. I knew all the actions but didn't know the Director. I could tell you all of the stories, but really didn't know the Author. Did I know that God had more? Sure I had heard it, but honestly I had never experienced it because I was satisfied with how much of Him I had.

> *I KNEW ALL THE ACTIONS BUT DIDN'T KNOW THE DIRECTOR.*
> #THEBURNFACTOR

I had settled for average.
I had settled for less, when God had more.
I had punched my one-way ticket to Heaven and that was about the extent of my faith. Not only had I settled for less, I had settled for straight up boring! Surely this wasn't the life Christ spoke of in John 10:10, when he said, "I have come that they may have life, and that they may have it

more abundantly." But this was where I was at in my faith, and the scary part was that I was content. One portion was fine for me. Wal-Mart had built an empire on the promise of "We Sell for Less"; I had built a makeshift faith on the premise of "settling for less."

How many of us stumble though life the same way? We get the whole God thing—we're down with that—but it's simply *a part* of our lives, instead of *being our lives!* We miss it! It's one piece of the puzzle, instead of being the entire thing. We fail to experience the true joy of surrendering all to Christ and going in with God all the way. We settle for less when God has more! We settle for one portion when God has two! Instead of experiencing the joys of drawing near to God and having him draw near to us (James 4:8), we settle for passively sitting on the sidelines of faith.

The Psalmist wrote in Psalm 115:14, "May the Lord give you increase more and more . . . ." Did you catch that? Not only is there more, but there is actually more and more! Double! We serve not only a God of more, but a God of more and more! I believe it is time we discover the God of more and more. The key is to discover. When we make an intentional decision to discover what it really means to know God and surrender all to Him, we find that there is so much more.

Jeremiah 29:13 says, "And you will seek Me and find Me, when you search for Me with all your heart." When we go all in and really seek Him, we find Him, and we find that there is more of Him to know and discover each and every day! That's what this book is about; it's about complete abandonment to God!

> **WE SERVE NOT ONLY A GOD OF MORE, BUT A GOD OF MORE AND MORE!**
> #THEBURNFACTOR

No half-heartedness.

No compromise.

No passivity.

A complete surrender.

CH1: IS THERE REALLY MORE?

A double portion of God's Spirit? Sounds odd, I thought to myself. Sounds strange, peculiar, almost ridiculous. Why? Little did I know, I was about to find out. I was about to discover the God of more and more.

CHAPTER 2

A STRANGE REQUEST

"And so it was, when they had crossed over, that Elijah said to Elisha, 'Ask! What may I do for you, before I am taken away from you?' Elisha said, 'Please let a double portion of your spirit be upon me'"
—2 Kings 2:9

Have you ever asked someone a question and had their answer completely catch you off guard? As a father of four young children, I feel like this happens almost daily.

"Hey, what are you guys doing in there?"

"What's in your mouth?"

"Why is your brother crying?"

"What in the world is that smell?"

I've experienced some amazing responses over the years from my kiddos, some that have left me absolutely speechless. One time when our oldest son Chase was two years old, he found some change lying around the house. Just an extra piece of parenting advice here, loose coins plus toddlers never ends well. We would take it away from him, but he always kept finding more. This exchange went on for a while and always left him utterly devastated when we took away his money! So after he came yet again with another coin, we decided to let him play with it for a few moments. And that ladies and gentleman is exactly how you should

NOT handle toddlers and pocket change. What a combination!

You've heard of the television show *Toddlers and Tiaras*; well, they've got nothing on kids and coins! We turned around and the coin was gone. "Chase, were did your money go, buddy?" we inquired. He would just look at us, eyes still watery from the last time we took away his precious treasure. After minutes of prodding and questioning, he finally responded in his toddler voice, "I wallowed it." "You did what?" we asked again, hoping we had misunderstood his toddler talk. He responded again this time a little louder and prouder, "I wallowed it!"

He was right. We discovered that we had properly named him Chase, and much like his counterpart, Chase Bank, he would happily stash away your money in a safe place! I still have the X-ray of the lodged coin hanging up in our garage. I jokingly remind him that I'm giving it to him on his eighteenth birthday along with the bill plus interest. Thanks to prayer and prune juice we discovered one of life's important lessons… this too, shall pass! Praise the Lord!

When I initially read Elisha's response to Elijah's question, it kind of caught me off guard, just like Chase's response did that day. Why would Elisha want a double portion? I mean, was one not enough? What was so different about Elisha? He seemed to be cut from a different mold then others. What an oddball! What a weirdo!

But maybe Elisha wasn't the weird dude after all. Maybe I was the one who was off kilter.

In the famous Sermon on the Mount, Jesus stated these powerful words, "Blessed are those who hunger and thirst for righteousness, For they shall be filled" (Matthew 5:6). In fact, all throughout Scripture, we find evidence of God's favor on those who are hungry for more of God. We see God respond to those who are desperate for more. I like to refer to it as a supernatural cause and effect.

The woman with the issue of blood was desperate to touch Jesus, and He responded.

The blind man refused to be silent crying out for mercy, and He responded.

Zaccheus climbed a tree when he was desperate to see Him, and He responded.

The woman broke her precious alabaster box, and He responded.

The paralytic's friends lowered him through the roof, and He responded.

Evidently Elisha knew the God of more, and he was not about to miss his opportunity to go all in and get a double portion!

THE NEW NORMAL

I believe it is time to redefine a new normal. I'm afraid that all too many of us are settling for a watered-down version of Christianity that leaves us looking at Elisha saying, "What a wacko!" You see, that's where I was. That's why this double portion thing had thrown me for a loop.

You mean, someone could actually like this stuff and want more?

The problem was that I had settled for the "stuff" and had yet to experience what it was like to abandon myself in full surrender to God. So when you've settled for a half-in, half-out type of faith like I had, you look at those pursuing God in reckless abandon like they're aliens from a different planet. In all reality, they are the normal ones. This happens all too often in our world today.

We hear of someone packing up and leaving the comforts of home for service on the mission field . . . our response? That's weird! We encounter the successful business person who walks away from that high-paying job and fat benefit package to pursue full-time ministry…our response? That's strange! "You're pursuing a Bachelor of Arts in Pastoral Studies? You're an oddball!"

When and where have we allowed this to become the exception and not the rule? We need a new normal. Elisha had tasted and seen that the Lord was good, and he was ready to do whatever it took to experience more of God. Perhaps the problem is that we have yet to truly experience what it is like to fully surrender to God, and as a result we are left with an altered life instead of an "altared" life.

When you alter something, by definition you make it different without changing it into something else[1]. Too often we settle for altering when what we really need is "altaring." The altar is a place of sacrifice: it is where something dies. The reason we look at Elisha and others who are living their lives in complete surrender to God and we see them as weird, is because we've experienced altering, but they experienced "altaring." We've become different without fully changing who we are; they went to the altar and completely surrendered. We look at them like they have three noses, but really we are the strange ones.

> **TOO OFTEN WE SETTLE FOR ALTERING WHEN WHAT WE REALLY NEED IS "ALTARING."**
> #THEBURNFACTOR

The apostle Paul said, "I beseech you therefore, brethren, by the mercies of God, that you present your bodies a living sacrifice, holy, acceptable to God, which is your reasonable service" (Romans 12:1). To paraphrase, Paul said, "Visit the altar and surrender all, because after all this is normal!" Going all in and completely sacrificing is not weird, strange, or odd . . . it is simply normal!

A TRUE FAN

I am a lifelong West Virginia University (WVU) Mountaineer fan. I'm not a casual or half-hearted band-wagon type of fan, but a genuine, die-hard fan. Before my children learned their ABC's, they could sing the WVU theme song, *Take Me Home, Country Roads*. Enough said!

Every year I try to attend at least one WVU game, and these have been some of the most fun and yet traumatic moments of my life, spent

CH2: A STRANGE REQUEST

with friends and family cheering on the old Gold and Blue! Yes, the word "traumatic" is not a misprint, for you see I don't handle losing very well, and needless to say, every game I've attended hasn't always ended in victory.

At one of the more traumatic moments, my wife and I were sitting beside Kenis, one of my lifelong best friends as we painfully watched the Mountaineers get destroyed by the Texas Longhorns on their home field in Austin, Texas. A good friend of ours had hooked us up with his season tickets, so at least one out of the three of us were thoroughly enjoying ourselves. Kenis was just as hard-core a Texas Longhorn fan as I was a Mountaineer fan, and he was living the dream, watching his 'Horns crush my Mountaineers.

Something happened during that game that I will never forget. Yes, my Mountaineers did get manhandled that day and I won't soon be forgetting that, I can guarantee it! But that isn't what is forever embedded in my psyche. What I will never forget is watching the difference between Kenis cheer on his Longhorns and watching the thousands of other Longhorn fans nearby cheer them on. There was quite a difference!

Kenis was a Longhorn fan on a whole other level. He didn't sit down or shut his mouth the entire game! In fact I still think to this day that I lost some of my hearing in my left ear as I sat beside him and listened to him holler!

He was straight up out of control. He was unashamed to cheer on his team with every ounce of energy and passion he had. I'll never forget as I occasionally glanced over and watched some of the "fans" around us in our section. They weren't like Kenis. Did they clap and cheer? Sure, but not like him. They were busy scrolling through their phones, clapping on occasion between bites of their hotdogs and nachos. Sure they had the team colors on, they looked the part, they knew the cheers, but you see, they weren't as committed as he was! Kenis was more than a fan, he was a follower. He was all in! I can still remember the "What a weirdo!"

glances Kenis got that day from the other UT "fans," as he stood and gave it all for his beloved Longhorns.

I couldn't help but think that many of us approach our faith the same way. We have the t-shirt, we know the songs, we attend the events, but has Christ really captured our hearts? Does He really have our full attention? Are we pursuing Him with everything we have? Or are we content with just one portion?

It's time we become spiritually like Kenis. Let's boldly live our faith in front of all the "fans" that are half-way committed and just along for the show. Let's redefine a new normal by going all in and completely surrendering all to the One who deserves it anyway!

BAD WATER

I must confess that I am a *Duck Dynasty* fan. Yes, along with millions of other fans, I caught the duck fever, became envious of those long beards and enjoyed watching the Robertson family. Maybe it was my southwest Virginia roots coming out of me? Maybe it was the man crush I had on the beards? I'm not really sure, but I enjoyed watching the episodes. Hands down, my favorite Duck Dynasty moment came in Season Two, Episode Seven. Uncle Si and the gang go out picking Muscadine berries, for Miss Kay to make her famous jelly. While filling his bucket, Uncle Si mistakenly picks up what he thinks to be a berry off of the ground and begins to eat it. He quickly finds out that it wasn't a berry at all, it was a raccoon turd!

I love this moment because I think it all too often depicts many people's response to faith and the things of God.

"Well, I've tried that, and it just wasn't for me."

"Yeah, my family was into that, and I know what it's all about."

"It's cool and all, but I'm not ready to get all radical and stuff."

Perhaps we've tasted the wrong berries? Have we really experienced what it's like to fully surrender to God and go all in? Or have we written

CH2: A STRANGE REQUEST

off God and faith, labeling those Elishas as "wackos," all because we've tasted the wrong berries? Have we really tasted the real thing? Think about it. Please excuse my graphic transparency here, but I'm sure there was "some" portion of Muscadine berry in that pile of Raccoon refuse. Too many of us settle, checking God off our list all because we've tasted a portion of God mixed with an abundance of other "stuff" that leaves us empty and searching for something else!

In John chapter four, Jesus has a very intriguing encounter in Samaria with a woman at a well. This lady's life was forever changed that day as He offered her a drink of Living Water, one that would never cause her to thirst again. The intriguing part is that she almost missed out on her miracle because of some bad water she had tasted. Upon his offer for Living Water, she at first basically responded with the "No thank you, Sir, I've tasted from this religious well, I know what it's all about, and I'm perfectly fine." Thousands of years before Silas Robertson ever saw the light of day, the woman at the well had beat him to the punch when it comes to feasting on refuse. She thought she had tried this Living Water, but she had never tasted the right thing. She had drunk from the religious well, leaving her broken, stumbling through life, searching for more.

> **SHE HAD DRUNK FROM THE RELIGIOUS WELL, LEAVING HER BROKEN, STUMBLING THROUGH LIFE, SEARCHING FOR MORE.**
> #THEBURNFACTOR

Much like the feelings I had when I read Elisha's strange request, I'm sure the Samaritan woman experienced similar emotions as she heard Jesus' offer that day at the well. "You mean people actually like this stuff? That's weird! That's odd!" It was because she had yet to experience what it was like to go all in and fully surrender! It all starts when we become open and honest before the Lord.

"Go and get your husband," Jesus told her. "I don't have a husband," the woman replied. Jesus said, "You're right! You don't have a husband—for you have had five husbands, and you aren't even married to the man you're living with now. You certainly spoke the truth!" (John 4:16-18) [insert #BOOM right there].

If we want to define a new normal, experience "altaring" instead of altering, and make Elisha's experience the rule and not the exception, it all starts when we become open and honest before the Lord.

Have you really tasted from the right well? Are you ready to go all in and experience life . . . not the life that you've always dreamed of, but the life that Christ died to give you? A life which I promise you will completely exceed all of your wildest dreams or imaginations!

I hear the Holy Spirit asking you a question right now, the same question posed by Elijah, "What may I do for you?"

Are you ready to respond? With His help, let's redefine a new normal in our lives!

CHAPTER 3

TAKE IT OR FORSAKE IT

"Jacob said, "First, swear to me." And he did it. On oath Esau traded away his rights as the firstborn. Jacob gave him bread and the stew of lentils. He ate and drank, got up and left. That's how Esau shrugged off his rights as the firstborn" —Genesis 25:33-34 (The Message)

I am the oldest of three children, with a sister in the middle, followed up by my brother. Along with every other oldest child, I would probably agree that there are inherent privileges that go along with being the firstborn. Let's just end the debate right now, there are privileges! For example, we get the "privilege" of being "test models" for our parents, as they learn how to handle these new life forms. By the time the second or third child comes around, parents have become pros at what to do and not to do, and the oldest child has the scars and marks to prove their theories!

And let's not forget the disciplinary side of the debate! Firstborns get away with nothing, nada, zip, zero, zilch! By the time the last child comes around, I think parents are just exhausted. I remember the first time I bleached or died my hair blond at age 13 at a fellow PK's (preacher's kid) house (you gotta watch out for those PKs, I tell you!). Even with having my Mother's permission to perform my first of many salon experiments, my Father, upon seeing my bleached head didn't talk to me for a week!

One whole week! My baby brother, on the other hand, had tattoos before he left high school! Tattoos! Now that might not seem like a big deal to some today, but in the late '90s in our circles, it was. No worries, Dad, I'm not bitter; my therapy sessions have helped tremendously! Ha!

In Bible times, there were most definitely benefits that came along with being the oldest son. Along with added dignity and power (Genesis 49:3), according to Mosaic Law, the birthright also included the rights to a double portion of the property to be inherited (Deuteronomy 21:17). So in this famous story, we find in Genesis 25 the rivalry between two brothers, Esau (the older) and Jacob (the younger). It is imperative to understand what was at stake.

Esau was essentially guaranteed a double portion with his birthright. It was his promise, his guarantee; he could take it to the bank because it belonged to him! Yet instead of pursuing the path and promises that were laid out for him, he forsook them.

I believe with all my heart that God has more for each and every single one of us! We've talked about this already in this book, but I do believe that God has more for us. You would have to be in an absolute spiritual coma to read the New Testament and not believe that God has more for us as followers of Christ who are fully surrendered to Him! I believe that God has a double portion of his Spirit set aside

> *IF YOU DON'T TAKE IT, YOU FORSAKE IT.*
> #THEBURNFACTOR

that He is willing and ready to pour out on all those who are willing to go after it. However, I must at this point enter the "Esau Clause" into the contract, which simply states, "If you don't take it, you forsake it." Esau had the double portion guaranteed as his, and he forsook it.

IRON CHEF

In this epic story that essentially changed the lives of both brothers forever, we find that Esau traded his double portion for some bread and stew. Jacob, the original "Iron Chef," was in the kitchen whipping up some of his famous red bean soup. I'm not sure if you can find Jacob's famous red bean soup recipe on Pinterest or not, but if you can, I would surely give it a try! Esau came in from the field absolutely exhausted and in a moment of weakness, sold his double portion for Jacob's stew. What a costly meal!

In one rash decision, Esau's life was forever changed as he allowed his fleshly appetite to overrule what should have been an easy choice. No! I will not forsake a double portion of what has been promised to me for one of your bowls of soup! I don't care how hungry I am, I'll find some cheese and crackers somewhere to hold me over! I don't care how good it smells or how nice it looks, it's not worth forsaking the promises I have for the future! How many times, though, do we choose what we see in the present, preferring pleasures over principles and promises?

We choose rash over right.

We choose beans over blessings.

We choose dumb over double.

Who in their right mind would forsake wealth, influence, power, and blessing all for the sake of a bowl of beans and bread? Sounds insane, but we see this every day. Daily choices determine our destiny. Often it's the simple one word answer of "Yes" or "No" that speaks absolute volumes about the path that we are on and what we are pursuing. Esau should have said "No" to Jacob's absurd request and to his own fleshly appetite and "Yes" to his future. You see, there is no middle ground here: you either take it, or forsake it.

Esau would have been a perfect case study for impact bias, which essentially is our tendency to overmagnify a current appetite and miscalculate how it will leave us feeling in the future[1]. Esau thought nothing else mattered at the current moment other than the fact that he was starving! This was his emotional state: "Look, I am about to die; so what is this birthright to me?" (Genesis 25:32). Esau was solely focused on one thing and one thing only.

Too often we allow the enemy of our souls to get us so caught up in what is happening that we become fixated on the wrong appetites and make absolutely stupid choices that affect our lives for years to come.

I'll never forget the year that the Sega Genesis video game console came out. I was so excited! This was absolutely groundbreaking technology. Suddenly, my Nintendo was not quite good enough anymore; I had to have the Sega Genesis! After all, the Sega controller would have three buttons, A, B, and C, making the A and B buttons on my Nintendo controller absolutely inadequate. My Mom wasn't seeing the big picture like I was. I was trying my best to state the case for why I needed this gaming console . . . it was a must! She said, "Son, this is just the newest thing right now. However, in a few months there will be another better one, then another, then another, etc., etc." I begged and pleaded with her stating, "Mom this is the BEST, there will NEVER be another gaming console any better! This one has three buttons!"

Mom was right. I was wrong. I was a strong case study for impact bias.

This is exactly where Esau was; he could only think of one thing: "I need this RIGHT NOW! I'm about to die, if I don't have this! This is a must!"

> **THE VOLUME OF THE NOW IS AT A MUCH HIGHER DECIBEL LEVEL THAN THE VOLUME OF THE FUTURE.**
>
> #THEBURNFACTOR

In these moments, our fleshly cravings and appetites become so loud that we struggle to hear any other voices and specifically the voice of the Holy Spirit. The volume of the NOW is at a much higher decibel level than the volume of the FUTURE. We need to allow the Holy Spirit to push the "Mute" button so we can stop for a moment and actually think about the choices we are making and refocus ourselves! Andy Stanley says, "Appetites always whisper *now* and never *later*." What would have happened if Esau hit the Mute button on his screaming appetite? How would history have changed for him? And for his family?

REFOCUS

The bottom line is that there is a double portion available for us that will forever affect our personal lives, our families, and the world in which we live. However, the choice is up to us whether we take it or forsake it. Will we allow the intensity of our fleshly appetites to be the driving force in our lives and decision making? Or will we allow the voice of the Holy Spirit and others that God has supernaturally placed in our lives to refrain and refocus us?

When Moses had his encounter with God at the burning bush on the backside of the desert, God revealed Himself to him saying, "I am the God of your father—the God of Abraham, the God of Isaac, and the God of Jacob" (Exodus 3:6). All throughout Scripture, this is the introduction line God uses and He repeats it, even to this day: "The God of Abraham, the God of Isaac and the God of Jacob." The job title on God's business card should read, "The God of Abraham, the God of Isaac, and the God of Esau."

You see, it's too bad that Esau didn't stop for a moment and refocus himself. It's a shame that nobody was there to come alongside him and help him see the lasting effect his choice was about to have on him and his future. It's too bad someone wasn't there to say, "Look, Esau I know you're starving, and I know those beans smell great, and I know that right now you feel like you're about to die, but just stop for a second and think about what you're doing!" This was his place. This was his part. This was his double portion. What could have been?

When I was 13, I had an experience with God at an altar at youth camp that forever changed the trajectory of my life. The service was winding down, and like a good church boy, I had already had some prayer time at the altar and was back at my seat, ready for the service to be dismissed. God was now far from my mind, and I was thinking about a cheeseburger, a snow cone, and shooting some hoops in the gym. Well, that's when my youth pastor, Nichole Syruws, tracked me down. I'll never forget that moment as long as I live. It was like she came out of nowhere, like Batman or something. She pointed her finger right in my face and with fire in her eyes she said, "Randy Lawrence, God is not done with you tonight, boy! He has more for you if you will go after it! Now get back up to the altar and seek Him!" Then boom, she was gone! And I was left with a choice.

You see, God used Pastor Nichole that night to help refocus me. She was an instrument of the Holy Spirit used to confront me on the spot and refocus me on God's plan for my life. Needless to say, I responded that night . . . Pastor Nichole was right! God did have much more for me. My life was forever changed, and I have never been the same since, because that night, I experienced the Baptism of the Holy Spirit.

HOLY ALARMS

Allow me to sound a spiritual alarm for you right now before we go any further in this book. Too often we look at stories like the one of Jacob and Esau, and we say to ourselves, "Well, I would never do that!" All throughout Scripture we read the stories, but feel certain we would never make those mistakes.

I would NEVER sell my birthright for beans.
I would NEVER betray Jesus for thirty pieces of silver.
I would NEVER fall asleep when Jesus needed me to pray.
I would NEVER deny Christ three times, not even once.

Not me! I wouldn't do that! I wouldn't lose my temper like Moses, break my promises like Samson, or commit adultery like David. But we do it every day with the decisions that we make. When we choose our ways over God's ways or our appetite over God's plan, we do the same! Daily decisions determine our destiny. What appetite are you allowing to be so loud in your life that it is taking precedence over God's promises and plans for you?

> **DAILY DECISIONS DETERMINE OUR DESTINY.**
> #THEBURNFACTOR

Are you ready for this? Don't you dare hit that snooze button! God has things to accomplish through your life that are beyond your wildest imagination. He wants to use you as a vessel through which He can impact generations for years to come, even long after you have left the earth.

There is a double portion available for you.

Yes, a double portion for you, but you must take it and not forsake it! God is no respecter of persons, and He desires to use you as His vessel to change the world! Today, hear God say, "I am the God of your Fathers, The God of Abraham, the God of Isaac and the God of (insert your name here)."

Allow the Holy Spirit to refocus you right now. What appetites in your life do you need to hit the mute button on? Which decibel levels of influence need to come down in your life because they are screaming NOW and not LATER?

Let the Holy Spirit refocus you right now because you are literally one choice away from a defining moment that will forever impact your life! Now is the time to make that choice!

SECTION 2

EMBRACE THE CALL

CHAPTER 4

BLINDSIDED

"So he departed from there, and found Elisha the son of Shaphat, who was plowing with twelve yoke of oxen before him, and he was with the twelfth. Then Elijah passed by him and threw his mantle on him"
—1 Kings 19:19

It was my freshmen year of high school, and our football team was suited up and ready for our first game. One of my jobs was to be the long snapper for the punt team. For those of you unfamiliar with the great game of football, the long snapper is responsible for "snapping" the ball back to the punter when a team is attempting to "punt" the ball away to the opposing team. Although long snappers play a vital job, they are typically overlooked or unseen, unless they screw up.

Fourth down came, and we were deep in our own end zone and forced to punt the ball from the half yard line. This made me extremely nervous; not only this, it was my first snap of the season! I remember staring over that ball, sweating it out, praying and hoping that I wouldn't mess up. I just knew in my mind I was going to snap it over the punter's head for a safety. The ready signal came from the punter, and I felt like my whole world stopped. I finally mustered the courage to snap the ball and hiked back the most beautiful long-snap a person would ever see.

I couldn't believe it.

"I did it!" "I actually did it!" I exclaimed! In fact, I was so excited and in awe of the fact that I had done my job, that I totally forgot that there was a very violent, brutal game still going on that we call football. So as I jubilantly jogged down the field after the punt, my victory lap was rudely interrupted by a member of the opposite team.

BAM!

I was left laid out on the ground seeing stars, Tweetie-Bird and Mario & Luigi. When I finally came to my senses, it was a real challenge for me to find my way back to my team's side of the field and a seat on the bench!

In football we call this "GETTING BLINDSIDED."

In 1 Kings 19, we read of one of the most classic BLINDSIDES in history. Elisha was going about his job, plowing the fields, living his life, and minding his own business, when out of nowhere, BOOM, he has this radical encounter! Elijah literally walks up to Elisha as he's plowing away, slaps his mantle on him, and then leaves!

You see, the mantle in Scripture represents many things; here it is symbolic of the prophetic call or gift that is on Elijah's life. Make no mistake about it, this was a clear-cut message that was being sent to Elisha. Often, this is how many of us experience the call of God on our lives. One day we are just out, minding our own business, living our lives, doing what we want to do, and—BOOM—we have this moment when we realize that we were created for more than just existing. We have a radical type of confrontation with God in which we realize that our life has purpose and He has a plan for us.

This type of encounter is a significant moment in one's life that must not be overlooked or undervalued. This holy collision is one in which heaven and earth seem to meet, and we encounter the divine set of plans that God has laid out for our lives.

All throughout Scripture we see these heavenly blindsides.

Noah was minding his own business, loving God, being a righteous man, when God gave him the seemingly overwhelming task of building an ark which would house two of every kind of animal on the face of the earth. Abram was living comfortably when God sent him some life-altering instructions, "Get out of your country, from your family and from your father's house to a land that I will show you" (Genesis 12:1). Moses was on the backside of the desert tending to his sheep when he encountered a burning bush and God began to speak to him. Peter was out on the lake, punching the clock as a fisherman, when Jesus invited him to leave his nets and fish to fish for men. Paul was on his way to kill more Christians when he was knocked to the ground and radically changed forever. The list goes on and on!

Do you get the picture? God loves these holy confrontations in which we encounter the fact that He has a purpose and a plan for our lives! You can't shake off these moments, these encounters; they stay with you for the rest of your life. You can't forget them, run from them or drown them out. No matter how you try to ignore them, these encounters with God are life-changing!

THE BIG PICTURE

As I sat there that day on the sidelines trying to recover from the brutal blindside hit I had taken, my coach came over and had some choice words for me. He grabbed me by the facemask, stared into my eyes and said (edited "PG" version), "Randy Lawrence, you better wake up, Son, there is a battle going on out on that field, and you just about got yourself killed!"

As I pondered his words and continued to try to remember my name and what planet I was on, I slowly began to realize a very important fact. The whole time I had been focusing on doing just one thing, snapping the ball—that was it. Now don't get me wrong, that was my primary role, but in the grand scheme of things I had failed to realize that I was out on the field for more than just that. I had more responsibilities and assignments on that one play than just snapping the ball. Our whole team had a job to do on that specific play, and I had more to do than to just snap the ball. I had failed to see the big picture and my lack of understanding had left me slobbering and half stupid, recovering on the sidelines.

I think this is how we often stroll through life. We find a place of comfort where we seemingly fit and stroll right through the stages of life, often failing to see the big picture. What is the big picture? It's the same thing that was slapped on Elisha that day in the field; it is the fact that God has a purpose and plan for our lives!

God has a calling on our lives.

I love how the prophet Jeremiah phrases this thought in Jeremiah 10:23: "I know, Lord, that our lives are not our own. We are not able to plan our own course" (NLT). This is a fundamental truth that is imperative for us to be blindsided by . . . God has a divine plan for our lives, a course, a destiny to be fulfilled. The Apostle Paul in writing to the church at Corinth asked them this question, "Don't you know that you are not your own?" (1 Corinthians 6:19). He's basically asking if they've been blindsided yet. Had they come to grips with the fact that they belong to God and that He has a plan for their lives?

I know right now that some of you might be thinking, "Yeah, OK, I got it. You're talking about those select few who have a call of God into ministry, like being a pastor or preacher or something." Well, let me blindside you with this: every single one of us has a call from God on our lives, and we all have unique giftings that He's given us. This mantle that has been placed on our lives requires that we come to grips with the fact that our lives are not our own and that God has uniquely created us in such a way to fulfill the purposes and plans that He has laid out for our lives.

First Peter 4:10 states, "As each one has received a gift, minister it to one another, as good stewards of the manifold grace of God." An integral

CH4: BLINDSIDED

part of being good stewards of the grace of God is being blindsided, then coming to grips with the fact that our lives are not our own and God has a purpose for us to fulfill.

There's not just a "select few" that God specially handpicks to use and then leaves the rest of us to sit and watch. Yes, we all have very unique callings, and yes, there are some who are gifted to serve in various roles that sometimes in the "Church World" seem more prominent than others. However, this doesn't change the fact that in the grand scheme of things we all have a part to play! The big picture is that there is a role for everyone and we need all hands on deck responding to this holy calling.

Life just doesn't seem to make much sense until we see the big picture showing us that we have a role or part to play in God's divine plan. We stumble through life much like the old school *Where's Waldo* books that show like a billion different faces on the page and everything's all cluttered and confused. But when the lights turn on and we see the big picture, we understand the words that God spoke to Jeremiah, "Before I formed you in the womb I knew you, before you were born I set you apart" (Jeremiah 1:5 NIV).

> **THERE'S NOT JUST A "SELECT FEW" THAT GOD SPECIALLY HANDPICKS TO USE AND THEN LEAVES THE REST OF US TO SIT AND WATCH.**
> *#THEBURNFACTOR*

When I was in junior high school, I participated in a few of our school theatre productions. What I always found fascinating was the level of emphasis that was placed on roles. Some parts were major roles, like the "star of the show," while others were very minor roles. During one production, I opted not to try out for any speaking or acting part, but instead became a stage hand and was left in charge of the curtain. Get this: I didn't have the leading role in the production, but if I didn't do my job, the audience wasn't going to see anything! Nada! I don't care how skilled or gifted our "lead" performers were, if I wasn't doing my job, we weren't going to be successful.

We all have a vital role to play in the Kingdom of God, and it is imperative that we are blindsided by and come to grips with the fact that He has placed His calling on our lives.

WHO ME?

Often when we are blindsided by the call of God on our lives, our response is simply, "Me?" The bottom line is that we struggle with the fact that God would actually choose us to use for his purposes and plan and we respond, "Not me God, You've got the wrong person!"

Gideon struggled with this same issue, that surely God would never choose him. In fact, when Gideon was blindsided with God's calling on his life, he responded to the angel delivering the message saying, "How can I save Israel? Indeed my clan is the weakest in Manasseh, and I am the least in my father's house" (Judges 6:15). *The Message* translation states Gideon's response as, "I'm the runt of the litter." Gideon's saying, "Like, um, sorry, Angel dude, I think your GPS has led you astray, and frankly, you've got the wrong guy!"

So many of us have this same response! We struggle with believing that God could or would actually use us. Moses had similar feelings and even came up with a long list of excuses as to WHY God shouldn't choose him. Isn't it just so awesome when we try to tell God what to do? NOT! You see, what happens is we get so caught up in thinking that God would never choose us that we begin believing things about ourselves that aren't even true!

Exodus 4:10 records Moses saying to the Lord, "I am not eloquent, neither before nor since You have spoken to Your servant; but I am slow of speech and slow of tongue." I find this to be a very intriguing statement from Moses, considering that Acts 7:22 states of Moses that he was " . . . learned in all the wisdom of the Egyptians, and was mighty

CH 4: BLINDSIDED

in words and deeds." How dangerously powerful our thoughts become when we argue with God over His calling! If we are not careful, we eventually place limitations on ourselves that in actuality do not exist.

On May 6, 1954, in Oxford, England, a man named Roger Bannister broke the world record by running a mile in Three minutes, 59.4 seconds. Roger was the first person in history to run the mile in under four minutes! What is so significant is that for years runners were told that this feat was seemingly impossible. These thoughts, over time, began to have a significant effect on the runners' ability to perform. Roger explained the barrier like this:

> *IF WE ARE NOT CAREFUL, WE EVENTUALLY PLACE LIMITATIONS ON OURSELVES THAT IN ACTUALITY DO NOT EXIST.*
> #THEBURNFACTOR

> The world record then was four minutes, 1.4 seconds, held by Sweden's Gunder Haegg. It had been stuck there for nine years, since 1945. It didn't seem logical to me, as a physiologist/doctor, that if you could run a mile in four minutes, one and a bit seconds, you couldn't break four minutes. But it had become a psychological as well as a physical barrier.[1]

With the breaking of the four-minute mile by Bannister, something shifted in the minds of other runners. They saw that it was possible to run a mile in under four minutes! The physiological barrier had been broken! In the next four years, 16 runners logged sub-four-minute miles.[2]

What thoughts about the call of God need to change in your life? Have you been blindsided yet? Or have you been trying to shake it off?

With the help of the Holy Spirit, I want to come alongside you today as Elijah came alongside Elisha and slap something on you. Here it is: there is a call of God on your life. No ifs, ands, or buts about it. It's real. It's genuine. There is a vital role for you to play!

No, God's not called the wrong person. You didn't accidentally pick up the wrong book. God has chosen you to help fulfill His purposes and plans in this generation!

CHAPTER 5

CHOICES

"Choose for yourselves this day whom you will serve" —Joshua 24:15

If you were to ever go out to eat with my side of the family, you would quickly find out something about us: we are very indecisive. In fact, I used to think we were indecisive, but now I'm not so sure anymore. OK, I'm sorry for the cheesy joke! But in all seriousness, my side of the family tends to be very indecisive on certain issues.

"Where do you want to eat?"

"I don't know, where do you want to go?"

"I don't know, you pick."

"No, you pick; I prefer you."

"Well, what's your favorite food?"

"I'm not sure, what's your favorite?"

These conversations can go on forever. When we are in new cities or locations (like on vacation), the indecision seems to magnify! Needless to say, it makes for some interesting family moments during days when we have to decide on more options than just where to eat. At some point, someone has to step up and make a choice! A choice. So simple, but yet so powerful!

Every day we are faced with choices. What to wear, what to eat, what to do, where to go, how to get there, and the list goes on and on. It has been said that the average adult makes over 35,000 decisions every single day![1] Try for a second to wrap your mind around that! Really, when you stop and think about it, our lives really take shape around the choices we make every day.

Much like a house is constructed, formed, and supported by thousands of pieces of lumber, our lives take shape and stand or fall as a result of the choices we make. First Peter 2:5 likens our spiritual lives to the construction of a home, "You also, as living stones, are being built up a spiritual house..." with Christ as the cornerstone or foundation of our structure. Day after day, our spiritual home is being erected by the choices we make. Simple choices put together over time create the framework of the spiritual house that we are becoming.

> **DAY AFTER DAY, OUR SPIRITUAL HOME IS BEING ERECTED BY THE CHOICES WE MAKE.**
> #THEBURNFACTOR

Think about this: we all start building our spiritual homes with the most incredible foundation ever, Christ as the Chief Cornerstone! He is the Foundation, and there is no better or any other way to build this structure. However, what makes or breaks us is what happens after this by the choices we make.

When Elisha is confronted with the call of God on his life, he is faced with a choice. He is brought to a crossroads where he must make a decision about how he is going to respond. What an amazing moment that must have been for Elisha that day in the field, basking in the fact that Elijah had chosen him and there was a God-ordained destiny for his life but, at some point he had to respond. He had to make a choice. He had to make an intentional move. God had made the first move and now it was Elisha's turn and a choice had to be made.

CH 5: CHOICES

DEER IN THE HEADLIGHTS

If you are old enough to drive, I'm sure at some point you've encountered a deer or multiple deer trying to cross the road that you are traveling down. Growing up in rural America, this vehicle vs. deer encounter was all too familiar. In fact, my father, who is an avid outdoorsman, bagged one of the finest bucks he'd ever seen with his '97 Buick! What makes the story even better (or worse, depending on how you look at it) is that he was on his way to the woods to go hunting!

I'm sure that if you've had one of these encounters with a deer, more than likely it happened when it was dark. It is absolutely amazing what happens to a deer when it encounters the brightness of your headlights. It's like a supernatural game of freeze tag. There stands a pretty elusive animal that can run up to 35 mph and clear a fence seven feet tall standing still, but when hit with your headlights, it is absolutely frozen![2] Biologists say that a deer's activity peaks typically within an hour or more before sunrise and sunset, so their vision is optimized for very low light. So when a bright headlight beam strikes their eyes, which are fully dilated to use as much light as possible, they are basically blinded, overwhelmed, and almost frozen until their eyes adjust.[3]

All too often in life we find ourselves like a deer in the headlights, especially when we have our initial encounter with God calling us. It's overwhelming in a sense to think that our lives have purpose and that God has chosen us. However, this divine encounter requires a response from us, and a choice must be made! We cannot stand there in awe of the moment forever; at some point we must take our next step!

In Acts 9, Saul had an incredible life-changing encounter with God on the road to Damascus. On his journey to kill more Christians, Saul was knocked off his horse by a blinding light, and God changed his life forever! In one moment, the trajectory of his life was permanently changed. Saul was left physically blind from his experience. There he sat on the ground, knocked off his horse, posing the first "deer in the headlights" look.

There is no way to explain this encounter in any other way than that it was absolutely divine! Such is our personal experience when we encounter God and His perfect plan for our lives. The same was true for Elisha that day in the field. At some point we must respond and do something!

What happens next is so crucial! The next step or move is, in all reality, one of the most defining moments on our journey with God and His divine plan for our life. Notice Saul's response, "So he, trembling and astonished, said, 'Lord, what do You want me to do?'" (Acts 9:6 NKJV). Saul made an immediate choice to stop what he was doing and ask the Lord what he should do next. With this simple eight-word sentence, we see a 180-degree turnaround in Saul's life. Saul takes the next step, makes a choice that defines the rest of his life, gets up off of the ground, and just like the Lord instructed him, he was led into the city and waited for further instructions. With this first crucial choice, we see the framework being put up in Saul's new spiritual house/life. What a journey it was for him!

THE CROSSROADS

God-encounters like Elisha had that day in the field and like the one that Saul experienced on the road to Damascus are really the crossroads of life. They bring us to a point at which we must make a choice. They serve as defining moments for our lives and for fulfilling the call that God has on us.

What is your next move?

How will you respond to what has just happened to you?

What will your spiritual house begin to look like?

As awesome as those God-moments are when we encounter Him and His plan for our lives, we can't just sit out in the barnyard, wearing our mantle, celebrating forever! At some point, we must take the next step. You see, Elisha was at a crossroads. He knew what this meant. He knew this signified that God had placed a calling on his life. He knew that this act by Elijah meant that there was a prophetic call or gift on his life, and it was an invitation to begin a life-changing journey, and I could go on and on, BUT ELISHA HAD TO MAKE A CHOICE!

God has a divine call on your life. He chose you, you didn't choose Him. You can't shake this, fake this, or make this. A foundation has been laid out, and before anyone walked the face of the earth, a divine blueprint was created which included you and me. Before you even took your first breath, a divine plan was created for you. With all of that said, God, in His loving nature, gives us a free will to make choices.

Please don't misunderstand me; He has done everything in His power to ensure that our spiritual home can be built up into an everlasting structure. Let me be very clear on this point . . . we can't do anything on our own. We can't earn it or change it because it's all done freely by His grace. However, we must understand that God gives us a choice.

What type of spiritual structure are you building with the daily choices you make? Specifically, as it relates to God's divine call on your life?

> **WHAT TYPE OF SPIRITUAL STRUCTURE ARE YOU BUILDING WITH THE DAILY CHOICES YOU MAKE?**
> #THEBURNFACTOR

Maybe you're like me and you have an incredible spiritual foundation; however, rather than make the choice to move to the next stage of construction, you just sit like I did on my blessed assurance, letting life pass on by. I was content to watch the other structures being built all around me while I stumbled through life with a feeling deep inside that I was missing something. At some point, we must make the move, and a choice must be made to pursue God's divine call.

Or perhaps you started the building phase and were off to a great start, but over the process of time, you've made some poor choices, choices that the enemy loves to throw up in your face to bring you shame. You see, the enemy wants you to scrap the building plans and abandon this journey altogether. He wants to pull you aside and whisper into your ear, "This is a mess, this house is falling apart and surely this isn't the plan for you."

It is in these moments when Satan loves to pull us off of the construction site and take us on a stroll through a different neighborhood. Here, seemingly magnificent homes exist, and he begins to entice us with alternative building plans. However, we know what lies behind these cheaply made homes without a solid foundation: a future of certain collapse.

We see this happen every day. I can take you to friend after friend from Bible College, men and women who were well on their way to being built up into magnificent spiritual structures. Somewhere along the way, they started making bad choices and listening to the wrong contractor. Today they are still stumbling through life, as they consider alternative building plans, searching for the right blueprints that they think will make them happy.

Maybe you started the building process and were off to a fabulous start but got injured along the way by those who were helping you build the house. Hurt and offense happen all too often from those we love, and it can be extremely painful. If you have never been let down, betrayed, or hurt by a fellow believer or a spiritual leader that you looked up to, then you evidently haven't been building very long. Jesus said to the disciples in Luke 17:1, "It is *impossible* that no offenses should come." Did you catch that? He said it is impossible to think that you won't be hurt or offended by someone on the same team. This *will* happen. We will be hurt by our fellow carpenter friends, and at these crucial moments in the building phase, we must make the choice to forgive and move on.

CH5: CHOICES

Here is the best news of all: God not only did everything possible to ensure our spiritual structure would be and could be complete, but then He sent us a Divine Contractor in the Person of the Holy Spirit. If you will open up your heart, the Holy Spirit's job is to come alongside you and assist you in this building process.

Even if you've made a series of bad choices, there's nothing He can't fix.

Even if you're just sitting on the job site in a sort of standstill, trying to decide whether or not it's worth it to continue, He can cause you to fall in love with the blueprints again.

He is here for you.

He was created for you.

You are not alone in this process.

The blueprints are laid out, and there is a divine call on your life. However, the hammer is in your hand and the choice is yours. What will you do next?

Allow the Holy Spirit to be your Divine Contractor and with His help, take the next step like Elisha did, and let's get this thing started!

CHAPTER 6
THE FIRST STEP

"Then Elijah passed by him and threw his mantle on him. And he left the oxen and ran after Elijah" —1 Kings 19:19-20

I still remember the place that I was standing that night in the Pensacola Civic Center when I finally decided that I was done with living my life on my terms. I was done with my passive faith. I was burnt out from sitting on the sidelines. I wanted to know the God I had read all about and experience Him for myself. I had finally come to grips with the fact that my life was not my own, and I was ready to surrender.

Even though I had heard all of the sermons, lessons, skits, and clichés on the divine plan that God had for my life, that night I came face to face with that divine call, and I faced a new choice that had to be made.

That was the moment everything changed for me. As I stood in that 10,000 seat arena attending the Elisha Generation Youth Conference, I suddenly realized why I never knew the God of more or about a double portion of God's Spirit, nor seemed the least bit interested in it. It was all because I had yet to take the step of fully surrendering my entire life to God.

I loved God—I really did—and I wanted to serve Him! I knew how to do all the right things and say all the right stuff, but yet there was a part of me that I had yet to surrender to Him. I was still holding on to certain areas of my life, specifically, my dreams, my future, and my plans. Did I love Him? Yes. But I had my own plans and my own dreams and had failed to recognize the fact that God wanted it all. He wanted everything. I realized that I wanted God on my terms rather than on His terms. He wanted it all. I wanted options.

> **I REALIZED THAT I WANTED GOD ON MY TERMS RATHER THAN ON HIS TERMS. HE WANTED IT ALL. I WANTED OPTIONS.**
> #THEBURNFACTOR

This is why I knew nothing of the God of the double portion, nor was interested in anything more than what I was content to experience on Sundays and Wednesdays. I had "just enough." But everything changed for me that night. I guarantee you I can still take you to the place in that massive arena where I was standing when I crossed the line and took the first step to go all in with God.

My encounter was in a civic center and Elisha's was in a farmyard, but both required a bold response. A holy "line in the sand" was drawn and a defining choice had to be made. I love Elisha's response: *he ran after Elijah!* He came to his holy crossroads and made the bold choice to run after the call of God on his life. He could have sat there in the pasture basking in the fact that God had called him. I'm sure it would have been an absolutely glorious time, but at some point he *had* to take the next step. Little did he know that as he turned to run after Elisha, that first step was defining a new journey that would forever change his life.

These divine encounters with God and the revelation of his calling are amazing experiences. All throughout Scripture we read of such supernatural events. We read of one in Genesis 28, where Jacob laid down his head to rest on a rock and literally a door of heaven opened and angels came up and down a stairway to him. He woke up, and I love his response, "How awesome is this place!" (Genesis 28:17). As I stood there in the Pensacola Civic Center experiencing my God-moment, it was almost as if I was having an out-of-body experience. I didn't see any angels like Jacob, but nonetheless it was just as equally a supernatural experience. Although I was surrounded by thousands of people, at that moment everyone was gone, and it was just me, God, and His divine call for my life.

As awesome as these moments are, we have to be careful not to get caught up in the power and emotions of the moment and fail to take that decisive first step in response to God's call. Elisha RAN after Elijah! Notice the very first thing he did was to take that first step in response to the call. It was a 180-degree turn from the life he had been living to the life that he was choosing to live from that moment forward. It was his moment of surrender. It was his moment of crossing the line. He left the oxen and ran towards his calling!

SET YOUR FOOT

On July 20, 1969, at 10:56 p.m. EDT, NASA Astronaut Neil Armstrong made history by planting the first human foot on another world. With more than a half a billion people watching this historic event on live television, Armstrong climbed down the ladder from the lunar module Eagle onto the surface of the Moon. As his foot touched the soil, Armstrong made one of the most famous statements in history, "That's one small step for a man, one giant leap for mankind."[1]

In all reality, as Armstrong stepped off of that ladder and onto the surface of the moon, it was just one simple step; however, what made that step so significant was what it represented. This step represented a new era in human history. It represented achievement, diligence, teamwork, commitment, and honor to those who had gone before and paved the way. An entire book could be written on what this one historic step represented.

One step.

I know it sounds so simple, but the importance of that first step of surrender and commitment to stop what you're doing with your life and walk in the direction of God's calling and divine plan cannot be overstated. It is literally history in the making. Armstrong took one small step on the moon. Elisha took one small step in the farmyard. I took one small step in the Pensacola Civic Center. One small step in the natural represented one giant leap in the spiritual. That first step is *so crucial!*

Steps are simple, yet steps are powerful. Steps seem insignificant, but they are monumental. God sees every step that we take, as Job 34:21 states, "For His eyes are on the ways of man, And He sees all his steps." What might seem like something that is so common and means absolutely nothing, means something in the eyes of God since He sees all of our steps.

That one step means something. It represents a shift.

As the children of Israel are on their journey to the Promised Land, God gives Moses a very unique promise in Deuteronomy 11:24, "Every place on which the sole of your foot treads shall be yours." Wait a minute, stop the presses, isn't the Promised Land already theirs? Now it seems like there is a new deal or condition, as God tells Moses that everywhere he sets his foot is his. Interpretation: Moses, you've got to take the steps, you've got to engage here with My divine call on your life and the people you are leading. Yes, I've promised it to you, and I'm going to be with you every step of the way, but you've got to have the courage to step into it. There will be milk

> **THAT ONE STEP MEANS SOMETHING. IT REPRESENTS A SHIFT.**
> #THEBURNFACTOR

CH6: THE FIRST STEP

and honey, but there will also be walls and giants.

Likewise, after Moses had passed on and his successor Joshua was on the scene, he encountered this unique characteristic of God as well. In Joshua 10, Joshua and the children of Israel set out to fight the five Amorite Kings. "So Joshua ascended from Gilgal, he and all the people of war with him, and all the mighty men of valor. And the Lord said to Joshua, 'Do not fear them, for I have delivered them into your hand; not a man of them shall stand before you'" (Joshua 10:7-8).

Joshua is given a solid promise of victory. AWESOME, AMAZING! But then look at the next verse and see how the plan had to unfold; *look at the STEPS that had to be taken.* "Joshua therefore came upon them suddenly, having marched all night from Gilgal" (Joshua 10:9).

Here's the promise: "Don't be afraid, I'm giving you the victory. Here's the plan, you've got to march all night from Gilgal." The march from Gilgal to Gibeon was no easy task. It was a trek of about twenty miles, which involved a climb of 3,300 feet and would have taken an entire night of hard, fast-paced marching.[2] Joshua led them on an all-night, brutal, fast-paced climb, all of this centuries before Red Bulls, Rockstars, and Five Hour Energy drinks! I mean some of us think P90X or cross training is intense, but they don't compare to Joshua's workout routine! Again, the plans had to be walked out, step by step.

In both stories we see a very important characteristic of God that we see all throughout Scripture: He loves to engage us in His plan, and it requires an action on our part. Yes, the plan is "sweet," but it will also require a lot of "sweat."

MOTION ACTIVATED

Today it seems as if everything has a motion detector. From cameras to lights to toys to vehicles, and of course, who could forget those annoying paper towel dispensers that never seem to work? (I promise I'm not bitter.) Did you know that red lights even have motion-detecting cameras? If you ever visit Los Angeles and have about $1,000 lying around that you'd like to donate to the city, you can experience this first hand and have an incredible picture for a keepsake! (Don't ask me how I know this.)

I swear that our youngest daughter Cali has a built-in motion detector. It doesn't matter how early in the morning I attempt to get up, she just senses human movement and BAM, she's awake! Many mornings as I attempted to get up hours before the rest of the household to try to write in the rare moments of silence, it wouldn't be long until I would feel a small tap on my shoulder and turn around to see those big brown eyes.

Please don't misunderstand what I'm about to say. We can't earn or work our way into something; the Bible is very clear on that. However, there are times when it feels like God has a supernatural motion detector, and He is waiting to see if we are ready to take a step. Does this mean we deserve anything or can work to earn something from God? Absolutely, one hundred percent NO. Our righteousness is like filthy rags. Even on my absolute best days I don't deserve God's love and compassion. I love the way author Tullian Tchividjian states it: Jesus + Nothing = Everything.

> **PETER SUPERNATURALLY WALKED ON THE WATER, BUT FIRST HE HAD TO TAKE A NATURAL STEP OUT OF THE BOAT.**
> #THEBURNFACTOR

With that understanding of God's grace, it is equally important that we see this characteristic of God that we read about in these stories and all throughout Scripture. James 4:8 encourages us, "Draw near to God and He will draw near to you." In a sense, God was saying, "Moses, I'm with you, but you must step out." "Joshua, the victory is yours, but you've got some marching to do." Peter supernaturally walked on the water, but first he had to take a natural step out of the boat. On and on, we see this displayed throughout Scripture. Matthew 7:7-8 says, "Ask, and it will be given to you; seek, and you will find; knock, and it will be opened to you."

So check this out. Here we have God, who is the only Being Who possesses omnipotence. The Oxford English Dictionary defines omnipotence as "all-powerfulness" or "almightiness."[3] Yet even though He has all capability and power, He chooses to use *us* to fulfill His plans. He uses our steps with His power. Our obedience meets His divine attributes and history is made!

He's watching . . . are you willing? There is a supernatural motion detector ready to be activated over your life as you take that first step and completely surrender to His purposes and plans. At the end of it all, you have one life to live and one life to give, so leave the oxen and run towards the call!

TAKE THE DIVE

A few years ago our family went out for a day on the lake with some of our best friends. Like most of our outings with this family, our day was filled with laughter, fun, and adventure, highlighted by an impromptu decision to go cliff jumping.

It didn't take too many dares, before the majority of the group dived off the boat and began swimming to begin our climb up the rocky cliffs. Once to the top of the cliff, the idea didn't seem to be as much fun as it had been a few minutes earlier as we looked at the cliff from the boat. However, one by one, we mustered the courage to jump off and take the plunge. It was frightening and fun all at the same time!

Once back in the boat, we realized that someone was not on board. We looked back to the top of the cliff to see one of our friends' daughters, still trying to muster the courage to take the leap. She wanted to with all of her heart. After all, she had already said "Yes" to the challenge, swam over to the cliff, and made the climb up. But now at the top, that jump seemed almost impossible in her mind.

This first step was one of complete surrender, leaving the comfort of the cliffs behind as she thrust her body into the air and trusted that she would land safely in the water below. Minutes passed by, and finally after almost an hour, she mustered up the courage to take that first step and jumped into the water below.

What is holding you back from taking that step? *It's just one step*...so simple, yet so significant. Take that step today with courage as you cross the line and leave the field and the oxen! Run after the call that God has placed on your life!

The whole time she was contemplating her plunge, we were exhorting her and cheering her on from the boat. Let me be that same voice to you today: "You've got this! God's hand and calling is on your life, so be brave and step into the life that He has for you!"

SECTION 3

BURN THE BACKUP

CHAPTER 7

NO PLAN B

"So Elisha turned back from him, and took a yoke of oxen and slaughtered them and boiled their flesh, using the oxen's equipment, and gave it to the people, and they ate" —1 Kings 19:2

I remember the first time I discovered the concept of a backup plan or "Plan B," as some would call it. I was in the fifth grade and was making final preparations for the big jump to middle school. One of the transition steps was the shift from music as a general education class that everyone took, to band as a specialized elective that only certain students participated in. As a part of this process, some students were selected or chosen to make the move to the band class. I was on that list and had to fill out some paperwork that would be passed on to the middle school band teacher for positioning and placement.

On that paper work, one of the questions was, "What is the instrument of your choice that you would like to play?" This was a no brainer for me. I wanted to play the drums, no question about it. I had always wanted to play the drums from a young age! Drummers were the center of attention, they were the real stars and I dreamed of my days of rocking the sticks.

"DRUMS," I spelled out in big, bold, fifth-grade letters.

Then I moved down to the next line, where I quickly became thoroughly confused. "What is your next instrument of choice?" Next instrument of choice? I thought to myself, "How is this possible? I only have one plan here and that is to play the drums!"

To this day I don't even remember the names of the other instruments I wrote down after the drums, because in my mind there was NO PLAN B!

To a PLAN A person, there is no such thing as a PLAN B.

After Elisha makes his choice to follow Elijah and respond to the call of God on his life, he makes another bold, decisive choice that had lasting effects on his life and ministry. The Scripture records that after receiving the invitation to follow Elijah, he returned to his plowing equipment, slaughtered the oxen, and cooked the meat with a fire that burned the plowing equipment!

Wow! Talk about making a statement. You could insert, "Drops mic, walks off stage!" right after this verse!

As bold a statement as this was, I believe for most people, upon casually reading this, it is difficult to grasp the significance of this moment; I'm afraid most of us don't. We read the sentence and move right along, failing to grasp what Elisha really did.

When I decided to follow the call of God on my life and go to Bible college, friends and family gathered to shower me with cards, gifts, and tons of packs of Ramen Noodles. This, however, isn't just a farewell barbecue for Elisha. Elisha doesn't slaughter the oxen and burn the plowing equipment just for amusement or recreation. A cold front had not come into Israel, causing Elisha to feel the need to start a fire. There is no singing of *Kum Ba Yah* and roasting of marshmallows at this bonfire.

This is a statement!

This is another crossroads on Elisha's journey. Every person eager to pursue the call of God on their life should learn from his example.

Elisha burned the backup plan!

This was Elisha's way of stating, "There is no plan B." This is Elisha's all-in moment with God, where he takes a bold stand and declares to his family, friends, himself, and to God that he is fully committed to pursuing the calling on his life.

LEAVE NO DOUBT

These oxen were more than pets, and the plowing equipment was more than common farm tools. These things symbolized Elisha's way of life. They represented his career, his way of making a living. The geographical region in which Elisha lived was known as an agricultural area. This, combined with the significant number of oxen Elisha was plowing with, indicate that he was more than likely a farmer, and a wealthy one at that. The Scripture indicates he even had servants tending the oxen along with him.

> **THIS WAS ELISHA'S WAY OF STATING, "THERE IS NO PLAN B."**
> #THEBURNFACTOR

So in essence, this move was Elisha saying, "I'm done with my days of farming; I'm giving it all up to pursue the call of God on my life."

Notice the commitment. He slaughtered the oxen.

Notice the passion and holy boldness. He used the plowing equipment as the firewood to cook the meat.

This was one bad dude. He wasn't playing around.

Too many of us go through life, leaving areas of doubt. We "patty-cake" around with the call of God He has placed upon our lives. We want to pursue God's calling on our lives and go all in, but there's a side of us that wants to hold on to things. Maybe it's a career, a dream, a habit, or a relationship. In all reality they become idols, because in the depths of our hearts we choose to hang on to these items to provide us a sense of security—or backup plan—failing to completely trust God.

We leave doubt.

I've been a lifelong fan of the West Virginia University Mountaineers. My father grew up in West Virginia, and if you know anyone from there, you know of the deep sense of heritage and pride shared among all those from that state. Without a professional sports team, West Virginians really rally around their state university; they have some of the most devoted fans in all of sports.

For Mountaineer fans like me, the 2007 football season is one that will forever be embedded in our hearts and minds. Coach Rich Rodriguez and his highly talented roster of players had led the team to a number two ranking in the nation, leading up to the last game of the season against border state rival, Pitt (The University of Pittsburg). Pitt was having a down year, and West Virginia was favored to win by almost four touchdowns. All of Mountaineer nation could sense that this was "our year."

Pitt came to WVU and won the game 13-9, leaving Mountaineer fans in shock and disbelief in what ESPNU called the "Game of the Year." To add to the pain of missing an almost certain chance to play for a National Championship, WVU Head Coach Rich Rodriguez accepted the head coaching job at Michigan shortly after the loss.

Assistant Coach Bill Stewart was named the interim coach and was given the daunting task of preparing the team to play against Oklahoma in the 2008 Fiesta Bowl. The number four-ranked Sooners were heavily picked to beat the now ninth-ranked Mountaineers. The Mountaineer players and fans from all over felt like their coach had walked out on them. This, coupled with the Pitt loss, had left the team emotionally devastated. Nearly every sports outlet, personality, fan, and oddsmaker had Oklahoma favored to win.

Before the game, interim coach Stewart gave a simple, yet emotionally charged speech to the team that is still talked about to this day. At the apex of the speech, Coach Stewart exhorted: "Let 'em know. Leave no doubt tonight! Leave NO DOUBT tonight! No doubt! They shouldn't have played the old Gold 'n' Blue. NOT THIS NIGHT! NOT THIS NIGHT!"[1]

After the speech, the Mountaineer players took his challenge seriously to "leave no doubt," and West Virginia defeated Oklahoma 48–28.[2]

Our unwillingness to go all in brings areas of doubt and uncertainty to our commitment to pursue God's call on our lives. God is calling us to go all in! Leave NO DOUBT! Burn the backup plan.

YES, BUT . . .

I can't tell you how many young people I've talked to over the years that want to fully commit to God's call on their life, but first they want to go after a sense of security that a job, career, or status appear to give. I have spoken many times with parents who know or sense God has a specific call on one their childrens' lives, but they want them first to pursue a career, degree, or certification. I've even met people who feel like they can only pursue the call of God on their lives after they first find their spouse.

When I hear this, my heart hurts. Is this really the type of life that God gave His Son up for us to have? Lives in which we feel the need to have our own manmade backup plans, just in case God doesn't know what He is doing?

It's almost humorous sometimes, how we feel the need to help God out, as if He doesn't know how to take care of every specific detail? We think that we need to help create a "Plan B" for Him.

Now let me clearly state, I'm not saying that pursuing careers or degrees are bad. Not at all! I'm grateful for the degrees I've earned. I'm thankful for the jobs that I've had. Neither am I saying that we can't have "secular" careers and pursue God's calling at the same time. Some of the greatest heroes of the faith we have today are those pastors, youth pastors, Sunday school teachers who work long, hard hours Monday-

Friday at their secular jobs and then fill the pulpits and classrooms on Sundays. They are much like Paul and Silas who were tent makers for a season in their ministries.

On the other hand, some of you know that the secular world is exactly where God has called you. And we need this! We need you to live out your faith and calling as a school teacher, doctor, politician, coach, and in other fields.

What I am saying though is that we should allow *absolutely nothing* to come before God and His divine call on our lives.

You see, these backup plans, whether they be a job, career, degree, or relationship, create a sense of false hope in our minds. We say to ourselves, "Well, if this God thing doesn't work out, I will always have the backup plan to fall back on."

In all reality, what we are saying is that our ultimate hope is in OUR plan, NOT HIS PLANS! We are saying, "Yes, God I know you've called me and I'm ready to respond, BUT…"

> **IN ALL REALITY, WHAT WE ARE SAYING IS THAT OUR ULTIMATE HOPE IS IN OUR PLAN, NOT HIS PLANS!**
> #THEBURNFACTOR

No matter how we try to slice it, what we are communicating to God is that we don't trust Him. But instead of facing this truth, we try so hard to spiritualize our stupidity.

"Well, I just need to use some wisdom here. You know I have bills to pay."

"God knows I've worked really hard to achieve this level in my career."

"I would be absolutely stupid to walk away from this."

Actually, we don't have the faith to fully surrender and say, "Yes, God, I trust You! You are THE PLAN." What do you have to lose? Sometimes we fail to remember the words of Jesus in Matthew 10:39, ". . . he who loses his life for My sake will find it."

CH7: NO PLAN B

I'm not trying to downplay the significance of these life-changing, difficult decisions. In fact, as I was typing the last sentence, I mistakenly spelled life-changing and typed "life-chafing!" Upon reading it I thought, "How appropriate!" These backup plans are often difficult to walk away from. Obeying God's call goes against every ounce of what our culture instills in us to do, and I'm not trying to downplay that.

What I am trying to do, however, through the help of the Holy Spirit, is to help you to see that you can trust God! His plan is better! I know it sounds crazy—even stupid—to walk away from that lucrative job or from an advancing career. The bottom line is this: if it's not crazy enough to scare you spitless and require faith, then perhaps you haven't heard from God or you're shooting too low!

"BACK THERE" MOVE

Growing up, I enjoyed watching wrestling. Before you cast judgment on me, this was back in the good ol' days of wrestling. I'm talking about the "Nature Boy" Rick Flair, "Macho Man" Randy Savage, Hulk Hogan, and my childhood hero, STING. Yes, I know it's fake, and rest assured I gave up the soap opera of wrestling years ago, but as a kid I loved it! My favorite part was learning the wrestlers' signature moves. "Nature Boy" Rick Flair had his figure-four leg lock, Hulk Hogan had the running leg drop, "Macho Man" Randy Savage had his diving elbow drop and who could forget STING's scorpion death lock! (I tremble even typing it!)

These signature moves defined these wrestlers. Let me help you with something. I've observed over the years a signature move of the enemy of our soul, Satan himself. He loves to direct our attention "back there." Unlike the signature moves of most wrestlers, signaled by a dramatic buildup (everyone knows they're coming), this stealthlike move of the enemy is very subtle. He loves to take our attention off God and complete trust in Him and turn our attention to "back there." He wants to make what God brought you out of seem like the place you need to return for refuge, shelter, or for an answer to your current problems.

This is clearly seen in Numbers 11, when the children of Israel begin to complain against Moses and focus their minds on going back to Egypt. "So the children of Israel also wept again and said: 'Who will give us meat to eat? We remember the fish which we ate freely in Egypt, the cucumbers, the melons, the leeks, the onions, and the garlic'" (11:4,5). Notice, all they mention is going back to all of the wonderful food, seemingly forgetting the slavery, abuse, and near-death circumstances that existed back in Egypt. The enemy's "back there" move was in full effect.

I think deep down inside, Elisha knew if he didn't go all in right up front, that the oxen would always be in the back of his mind. "Well, if this prophet thing doesn't work out, I can always go back to farming."

> **WHAT BACKUP PLANS DO YOU NEED TO BURN?**
> *#THEBURNFACTOR*

Not only would it forever remain in his mind, but the enemy would love to come and present "Plan B" in the difficult and trying times to remind him of the lucrative job waiting back home.

You see, the enemy absolutely loves to do that; it's one of his favorite moves.

Elisha took care of this right up front. He burned the backup plan. There was absolutely nothing for him to fall back on. No Plan B. No other option. It was all God and nothing else!

What backup plans do you need to burn?

Fill in the blank:_____.

What is it that you have said in your heart, "Well I just need to keep _____, or I just need to have _____ first, then I can pursue God's call."

Just over a century ago, a brave group of missionaries helped pave the way for the gospel on many foreign soils. This bold group essentially became known as the "One Way Missionaries." They essentially

CH7: NO PLAN B

purchased a one-way ticket to the field they were called to with no other plans or return tickets. These pioneers often packed their belongings not in suitcases, but in coffins. There was no Plan B.

It's time to go all in.
It's time to make a statement.
It's time to burn something.

CHAPTER 8

OUT OF THE COMFORT ZONE

"Sometimes the danger of missing out is greater than the risk that comes with stepping out." —Steven Furtick

Growing up, I was terrified of heights. I have no idea why. I can't explain it or pinpoint it, but I was just always afraid of them. I still remember as a young child when our family visited the Grand Canyon, how difficult it was for me to get anywhere remotely close to the edge to take a look. My brother and sister would go and stand right on the ledge and it would just absolutely freak me out!

So when I was 17 years old and at an amusement park with many of our family members, I was shocked when my two crazy uncles were able to talk me into going on an extreme flying ride. This ride, for which you had to sign waivers, was much like bungee jumping. You were dropped from an extremely high height and left free falling until the cords caught you and swung your body out in a circular motion just before you hit the ground.

To this day, I don't know why I agreed to do it. I think it was because I wasn't man enough to confess to my uncles that I was scared to death to do it. On the other hand, they were offering to pay for it as a graduation gift. Since I have a horrible time saying "No" to people, I agreed. After signing waivers and getting strapped up in our suits, we were hoisted higher than I ever imagined above planet Earth. I wasn't quite sure if I was going to survive. The higher we went, more of my life flashed before my eyes. Then came the worst part; after getting to the top, my uncles informed me that they had arranged it so that I was the only one who could pull the release cord.

I thought, "Are you serious? It's bad enough that I'm the only one that is deathly scared of heights, and now I have to be the one that pulls the release cord, sending us free-falling down to planet Earth?" Needless to say, it took me a while, but at some point, I had to face my fears and muster up the courage to pull the cord.

Looking back at this adventure, I can honestly say this is one of the best things I have ever done. Why? Forget the fact that it was exhilarating beyond belief and terrifyingly fun. What made it one of the best things I've ever done was the fact that I faced my fears and got out of my comfort zone.

When Elisha made his bold move to burn his backup plan, you can rest assured it was a move outside of his comfort zone. This was not your average barbecue; this was a costly move by Elisha. As previously pointed out, the large number of oxen Elisha was plowing with make it apparent that his family were very wealthy farmers. Author and pastor Mark Batterson wrote the following of Elisha:

> Most family farms were small enterprises consisting of a single plow with one set of oxen. Having twelve yoke of oxen, along with the farmhands to plow with them, is evidence that Elisha came from wealth. And it was all his to inherit. Burning the plowing equipment was more than quitting this job. It meant divesting himself of his share in the family.[1]

CH8: OUT OF THE COMFORT ZONE

Elisha forsook everything, willing to lay it all on the line. You see a radical call requires a radical response and commitment! Elisha was ready to step out of his comfort zone and pursue the call of God on his life.

OUT OF TOWN

I like to consider myself a person that pays attention to details . . . or at least I try to be a person who does! I love the details that we see all throughout Scripture. Sometimes, however, we read right over simple details without stopping to think about their significance. One such occasion is found in the story of the blind man who receives his sight in Mark 8. The Scripture records the following narrative:

> Then He came to Bethsaida; and they brought a blind man to Him, and begged Him to touch him. So He took the blind man by the hand and led him out of the town. And when He had spit on his eyes and put His hands on him, He asked him if he saw anything. And he looked up and said, "I see men like trees, walking." Then He put His hands on his eyes again and made him look up. And he was restored and saw everyone clearly (Mark 8:22-25).

We often read this story and the first thing that stands out in our mind—other than the fact that the blind man was healed—is the method Jesus used. He spit in the dude's eyes! Wow! Anyway, if you look past the "Holy Spit," I think the "Holy Spirit" has some important details for us in verse 23. "So He took the blind man by the hand *and led him out of the town*" (emphasis added). We often read right over this part, because we are focused on the exciting part in the story in which Jesus heals the man's vision by spitting in his eyes! However to me, the real miracle doesn't happen in verse 25; the real miracle starts in verse 23 when the blind man is led out of town.

Think about this: why would Jesus feel the need to lead the blind man out of town? After all this is the Son of God, and He can do anything, right? Correct, He can do anything, anytime, anywhere He wants. So why did He first lead him out of town? What is significant about this small but yet important detail?

I believe the significance is that sometimes Jesus wants to see if we really want what we say we want. Sometimes God just wants to know if we are we willing to get out of our comfort zone.

This is a man who has been blind. For him to leave town means that he has to be willing to step out of his comfort zone, away from familiar territory. You see, if you've ever watched or been around a blind person, you know that they memorize or are familiar with their surroundings. It becomes a comfort zone for them. They know that there are ten steps to the refrigerator, five steps to the bathroom; you get the idea. Their surroundings are their comfort zone.

> **SOMETIMES JESUS WANTS TO SEE IF WE REALLY WANT WHAT WE SAY WE WANT.**
> #THEBURNFACTOR

So when Jesus leads this man out of town, it is a big deal for this guy! He is stepping out of his comfort zone, away from everything familiar. He's leaving his beggar friends back on the street corner where he's lived his entire life. He was comfortable there.

Now let me ask you a question: Where does the miracle happen?

Answer: out of town!

The miracle happens as the man leaves his comfort zone and steps out into unfamiliar territory, bravely following Jesus! The call of God on our lives demands that we step out of our comfort zones and have the guts to follow Jesus into the unknown.

BOAT OR BRAVE?

Peter always gets flack for being the one who took his eyes off Jesus and started to sink; too often we overlook *the fact that he did walk on water!* Let me say that again, HE DID WALK ON WATER! Jesus offered the invitation to any of the disciples to come to Him out on the water, but only one responded, Peter. He was the only one willing to step out of his comfort zone, leave the safety of the boat, and step out in faith to follow Jesus.

Peter stepped out.

He was bold.

He was willing.

Yes, he sank, but his motives were pure as he stepped out of his comfort zone to respond to the call of Jesus. The others just sat there in the safety of the boat. It's better to fail trying to step out and follow God than it is to sit safely in the confines of the boat. A wet booty is better than a numb booty any day of the week when your chasing after God's call!

I find it to be no coincidence that when Jesus had to choose someone to lead the Church, He chose Peter. Peter was the one who was willing to get out of his comfort zone. He wasn't better than everyone else, but he was braver than everyone else. It was Peter, the one who, when everyone was content to sit on their blessed assurances, was willing to bravely jump out of the boat and follow his Savior. Today it is no different. When God is looking for someone that He can use mightily, He looks for those who are willing to get out of their comfort zone and go all in and all out for Him.

Noah looked like a fool as he worked for decades building the ark.

Abram left the comfort of home and family as he set out on a journey to follow God.

David left the safety of the sidelines to fight the giant.

Benaiah chased a lion into a pit on a snowy day (sounds backwards, but it's correct).

Mary Magdalene broke the costly bottle of perfume.

Stephen gave his very life, his last breath.

We see this common thread run not only all throughout Scripture, but all throughout Church history, even to this very day.

> **JESUS TAKES NOTE OF THOSE WHO ARE WILLING TO BURN THE OXEN.**
> #THEBURNFACTOR

Jesus takes note of those who are willing to burn the oxen. He notices those who are willing to leave the safety of the boat. God's calling on our life requires that we be willing to step out of our comfort zones and leave the safety of our surroundings to pursue His divine call.

How many times do we miss out on what God has for our lives due to our unwillingness to commit ourselves to God beyond our comfort zones? We cry out at the altar, "God use me, here's my life, anything for You," but then we fail to have the "walk" that matches our "talk."

Just as I was finishing up this section, my youngest daughter, Cali, came and tapped me on the shoulder and handed me an envelope. She said, "Daddy, I made something for you, it is a special gift! Open it!" she insisted jubilantly. I stopped typing and turned my attention to her and her special gift. Opening the envelope, I found a coloring sheet that she had ripped out of a coloring book. As I pulled it out, she exclaimed, "I made it just for you!"

As I scanned over both sides of the paper, there was not one hint of color anywhere. Not one smudge of crayon was to be found! I replied, "Cali, thank you so much for my special gift," giving her a big hug, "but I don't see where you colored anywhere on it, Sweetheart."

Not fazed at all by my inquiry, she just smiled and replied, "I know Daddy! I know! And I made it just for you!"

How many times in life do we do the same when it comes to our response to God's call on our lives? We say, "I give you my life, God, it's Yours! I give you everything!" But in reality, we know that we are holding back certain areas, unwilling to go all in, thinking, "Well, I can always go back to this or that...." Grand promises, but bland commitments.

BURN THE SHIPS

In the year 1519, Spanish conquistador Hernán Cortés landed on the peninsula of Mexico and set out to conquer the Aztec empire. Arriving with 11 ships and more than 500 men, Cortés faced a giant task in trying to overcome the Aztec empire. Many had tried before and failed. Here on the shores, legend has it that Cortes issued a bold order that would change the destiny of his mission: "Burn the Ships."[2]

This move to destroy the ships was more than a bold plan; it was an all-out commitment. As Cortés and his army watched the remnants of their ships sink, the comforts of home and the possibility of retreat dissipated as well. This was their moment of complete surrender to the task at hand.

What is it today that is holding you back from going all in? What is it that is keeping you from stepping out of your comfort zone and pursuing the call of God on your life with reckless abandon?

Now is your moment to step out. Have the courage to push past your comfort zone and bravely step out in pursuit of what God has called you to do!

A few weekends ago, our family was crammed into a small gymnasium watching our seven-year-old son Chase play a basketball game. Chase is a great competitor. He loves to compete and play the game regardless of the sport. While he is blessed with some athletic skills, he may not always be the most talented or gifted athlete on the field or floor. However, you rarely find a kid that tries harder or is more committed. Such was the case on this day in which he was all over the gym. He was diving left and right, sliding all over the floor, and chasing after every loose ball. You would have never known this was the YMCA league and they didn't even keep score.

As we walked out of the gym that day, I took a look down at Chase's knees, which were beet red with some "really nice" floor burns. I pointed them out to Chase and asked, "Son, do you see your knees? Do you know why they are so red and probably hurt right now? It's because you have a floor burn. Son, you have what we call 'skin in the game!' (Cue the *Braveheart* soundtrack music here!) You left it all on the court out there today, son! You hustled, you gave it your all! You sacrificed your body for the sake of the team! I'm so proud of you, son."

We are called to so much more than a recreational game of YMCA hoops. We have a God-ordained destiny and calling on our lives that is waiting to be fulfilled! It's time to step out of our comfort zone and get some skin in the game!

CHAPTER 9

THE BURN FACTOR

""The world has yet to see what God can do with a man fully consecrated to Him." —D.L. Moody

Have you ever encountered a Christian that was just different from other believers? When they talk about Christ, it's different. When they worship, there seems to be more passion. When they pray, it seems as if Christ is right in the room.

They almost have a holy edge about them.

What is it about these followers of Christ that is unique? What attribute do they possess that makes you say, "There's something different about them! I want what they have!"

As you encounter these individuals, you feel inspired to love and pursue after God in a way you never dreamed possible.

They possess what I call "The Burn Factor."

They stand in a long line of brave followers of Christ like Elisha, people who were willing to fully consecrate their lives to the pursuit of God's call. They boldly said, "YES," became fully committed, burned the backup plan, and never looked back.

During my freshman year of Bible college in Pensacola, Florida, I met Sudip Khadka. Sudip came to the U.S. from Nepal, where he had lived his entire life, solely to attend Bible college. Obviously, coming from a foreign country and experiencing the United States for the first time, many things stood out about Sudip. However, the first thing that quickly became apparent to me was that Sudip possessed the Burn Factor.

I can honestly say that after encountering Sudip and his commitment to Christ, my life has never been the same.

Sudip was born and brought up in an Orthodox Hindu family in Nepal. Being the first male born in the family after six females, his arrival brought great hope to his father, who was heavily involved in politics and was also a witch doctor. At the age of 11, a gentleman shared the gospel with Sudip and he received Christ. After becoming a believer, Sudip was kicked out of his home by his father because of his faith and went to live in an orphanage. Sudip experienced rejection and persecution much of his early life, as Christianity was illegal in Nepal. At the age of 15, Sudip's spiritual father who had led him to the Lord, was thrown in prison for his faith, leaving Sudip to lead the local church congregation.[1]

Sudip could have talked for hours about the miracles he had seen in his life. But that wasn't what captivated me. Cool, yes, but that wasn't what stood out. It was his deep commitment to follow God's call on his life, regardless of the cost, that caused him to stand out in the crowd. I had over 1,500 fellow students that semester all in love with Jesus and committed to following His plan for their life and in pursuit of ministry, but Sudip was different.

He had the Burn Factor.

He knew what it was like to go all in with Christ, to burn the backup plan and run 110% in the direction of God's call, absolutely never looking back. He, like Elisha, knew what it meant to make a choice in life and never look back, no matter how difficult or hard the situation might be. He was committed. He was all in. He had the Burn Factor and everyone that encountered him knew it.

CH9: THE BURN FACTOR

All through Scripture and history we read of these bold followers of Christ who possessed the Burn Factor. Hopefully, you've met someone in life who had it, and if so, you can attest that these people leave you inspired to follow Christ in a way you never dreamed possible.

Like Elisha's bold move that day in the farmyard, it's their commitment and consecration to the call that sets them apart. That is the Burn Factor.

It is what separates the casual from the committed and the fan from the follower.

These followers of Christ are history makers. They have paved the way for the gospel all across the globe. They have planted churches, schools, orphanages, and missions. They have rescued innocent children caught up in human trafficking. They have carried the gospel to unreached tribes and villages. They have gone where others have dared not go.

They have also taught school, run law firms, played professional sports, and led multi-billion dollar corporations. They have changed the world, one life at a time.

Not only have they shaped history, but they continue to do so to this day.

It's all because they said yes to the call of God and never, ever looked back, not for one moment. They have the Burn Factor.

They preach differently.
They work differently.
They talk differently.
They worship differently.
They give differently.
They live differently.

There is a holy edge on their life that causes them to stand out in a crowd.

Don't be confused; these are common, everyday people. They come from all walks of life and different socio-

> *IT'S THEIR COMMITMENT AND CONSECRATION TO THE CALL THAT SETS THEM APART. THAT IS THE BURN FACTOR.*
> #THEBURNFACTOR

economic backgrounds. They are young and they are old. What's the common denominator?

They all said YES.

NO FOOL

On January 2, 1956, 29-year-old Jim Elliot set out on a journey that would forever change the destiny of an entire people group. Almost three years of jungle ministry and hours of planning, praying, and preparation had led him to this day. He, with four other missionary friends, Ed McCully, Roger Youderian, Nate Saint, and Pete Fleming had set out on a short flight over the thick Ecuadoran jungle to set up camp in the territory of an extremely dangerous and uncivilized Indian tribe known then as the Aucas, today known as the Waodani tribe.

The danger of this endeavor was evident by the fact that the Aucas had killed all outsiders caught in their area. But Jim knew that he must share Christ with this unreached people group. Six short days after being dropped off on the Auca beach, all five of these heroic missionaries were speared to death by the Auca Indians. They had yet to win even one of these tribal members to Christ. Through natural eyes, this seemed like such a tragic loss. However, a few years earlier, on October 28, 1949, Jim had written in his personal journal, "He is no fool who gives what he cannot keep to gain that which he cannot lose."[2] The Aucas didn't take these missionary lives, because these men had given them up long ago when they said "Yes" to the call.

The story doesn't end here. In less than two years, Jim's widow, Elisabeth, and her daughter Valerie, as well as Nate Saint's sister, Rachel, moved back into the Auca village to continue the mission of reaching this tribe. Many Aucas became Christians, and to this day the tribe has been radically changed due to the obedience of these brave missionaries.[3]

They had the Burn Factor.

You see, the Burn Factor pushes us past our comfort zones and positions us to be used by God in ways that we could never imagine. It gives us the strength to do hard things, knowing that we are pursuing nothing else but God and His plans.

Only those who are "all in" possess this distinct factor upon their lives.

After returning home from my trip to the Elisha Generation youth conference, I knew that I was forever ruined for a normal life. I had come face to face with God and His call on my life, and I made the choice to say, "Yes! Yes God, I will follow You wherever you ask me to go and do whatever You ask me to do: my life is Yours."

> **THE BURN FACTOR PUSHES US PAST OUR COMFORT ZONES AND POSITIONS US TO BE USED BY GOD IN WAYS THAT WE COULD NEVER IMAGINE.**
> #THEBURNFACTOR

I was hungry to follow His ways and desperate for more of Him in my life. I can still remember the van ride home from Florida with the fire of God burning in my heart. I wanted a double portion of God's Spirit.

I can honestly say that God radically transformed my life, and the more that I sought after Him, the more He continued to pour into me. I couldn't get enough of Him. People began to notice the transformation. I was determined to follow God's call and was committed to making daily decisions that would determine the destiny God had assigned me.

My bedroom was transformed into the most awesome place, a place where I would daily meet with God! I still remember pacing circles around my ping-pong table, learning how to pray and seek God. Often, when many of my peers were out at social events, I would find myself in my room, praying and worshiping God. My walls became covered with passages of Scripture and reminders of the calling of God on my life.

I literally was a new person. I was on fire and there was no looking back.

People began to take notice. A month later after returning home, I attended church camp where a very well-known national youth speaker was speaking for the second straight year. I specifically remember on the last night that he pulled me aside to pray for me, saying, "Randy, in all of my years of ministry, I can't ever remember seeing such a drastic change in a person."

About six weeks later I returned to high school for my junior year. Immediately, I had students come up to me that I had known my entire life and ask me what my name was! Now listen, this wasn't because I had been living this awful, sinful, dirty life; it was simply because I had said, "Yes, God I'm willing to go all in with You," and He had radically changed me!

I had the Burn Factor! I said "Yes" to the call, consecrated my life, and burned the backup plan. There was no looking back.

FULLY CONSECRATED

If you're familiar with Church History, surely you've heard of Dwight L. Moody. Moody was a poorly educated shoe salesman who felt the call of God to preach the gospel and was mightily used by God. He became one of the great evangelists of modern times and founded Moody Bible Institute in Chicago, Illinois, which is still impacting lives to this very day.

God used this ordinary man to do very extraordinary things all because he said "Yes." Early in his ministry, Moody's friend Henry Varley said to him, "The world has yet to see what God can do with a man fully consecrated to him." In response to this comment, Moody made the commitment, "By God's help, I aim to be that man."

It is estimated that over his life, Moody preached to 100 million people and clearly left his imprint on the world.[4]

A few years after Moody's death at a memorial service, Evangelist R.A. Torrey, who had been one of his closest friends, said,

CH9: THE BURN FACTOR

> The first thing that accounts for God's using D.L. Moody so mightily was that he was a fully surrendered man. Every ounce of that two-hundred-and-eighty-pound body of his belonged to God; everything he was and everything he had, belonged wholly to God.[5]

Moody set out to be that man, the man who would be willing to fully consecrate everything, and he shaped history.

He had the Burn Factor.

Today, even as you are reading these words, cities are waiting to be transformed. Schools are ready to be impacted. Communities and villages all across the globe are ready for life-change. What are they waiting for?

They are waiting for men and women to fully consecrate themselves to God's plan! They are waiting for those who are willing to go all in, burn the backup plan, and fully consecrate their lives to God. By the grace of God, let's be those men or women!

Be determined today that nothing is going to stand between you and the call of God. You have only one life to live and one life to give.

> **BE DETERMINED TODAY THAT NOTHING IS GOING TO STAND BETWEEN YOU AND THE CALL OF GOD.**
> #THEBURNFACTOR

Fully consecrated, fully committed.

In the words of missionary William Borden, who gave his life for the spread of the gospel, "No reserves, no retreats, no regrets."

Do you have it?

Do you have the Burn Factor?

If not, may I remind you right now, in this very moment, that God is

NO RESPECTER OF PERSONS! Translation: You can have it! You can experience the Burn Factor, cross the line and go all in today!

SECTION 4

START NOW

CHAPTER 10

HOLY HUSTLE

"Then he arose and followed Elijah" —1 Kings 19:21

There's no mistaking just how incredible a God-encounter is. The encounter that Elisha had that day in the field was one that would mark him for the rest of his life. My personal encounter in the Pensacola Civic Center where I came face to face with God and His divine call is something I will never forget.

However, often when a person experiences such an encounter with God, he or she struggles to build the bridge from this supernatural experience with God to actually walking out His call on his or her life. To put it simply, they struggle as they come off of the emotional high as they take the next steps.

They hear God's voice calling them to go a specific direction, so they consecrate themselves and go all in. There is often this space or gap that appears that, if not handled correctly, causes individuals to get frustrated, or worse yet, to retreat.

If you've ever been over to the United Kingdom and have experienced riding on their public transit system, you will have noticed a sign posted with words that at first seem a little odd. Down in the subway, as you prepare to step onto the train, on the floor in big bold letters there is a sign that reads "MIND THE GAP." As an American, it seems a little odd, because it doesn't sound right to us. "MIND THE GAP" just sounds weird (no offense to my British friends), but nonetheless, you must understand the vital message being communicated.

There is a gap between the platform and the train and you absolutely need to pay attention to it! If you don't, there will surely be problems, and you will fall and end up on one of those classic *Youtube* videos somewhere that bring us all joy.

MIND THE GAP.

Yes, you have your ticket, you know where you're headed, and you're in the right station, but as you prepare to step onto the next train, you must pay attention to the GAP. So many of us struggle with the GAP!

PUTTING THE PIECES TOGETHER

I compare this common struggle to purchasing something from IKEA. IKEA is an amazing home furnishing store found across the U.S. and throughout the world. If you've ever been in an IKEA, you know that just walking through one is an experience in itself. They sell some of the coolest, most unique home furnishings you can possibly imagine. But their meatballs are terrible (#justsaying).

I remember the first time we bought something from IKEA. We saw a particular item in the store and were just absolutely mesmerized by it (if you've been to IKEA, you totally understand). The price was shockingly low, so we grabbed it! I remember getting home and being so excited to add our new furnishing to our home and show it off to all of our friends. And then came the problem: trying to read IKEA's instructions! They were virtually impossible to understand! There were all these weird pictures and no words, I was completely lost, confused, and disoriented!

CH10: HOLY HUSTLE

I remember just sitting there, holding the furniture parts in my hand, thinking, "What now?" The awesome encounter and dream of filling my home with such a fine piece of furniture seemed all but a distant memory! It looked so awesome in the store, but all I was left with was frustration and feeling like I wanted to give up.

This is how so many of us feel after our mountaintop experience with God and His call. We have this incredible God-encounter at a camp, conference, or meeting, but then WHAT? We struggle with putting the pieces together and determining what to do next. It is imperative that we learn from Elisha's example and pay close attention to just exactly what he did in this situation.

The Scripture says, that " . . . he arose and followed Elijah." Notice that Elisha wasted NO TIME. He immediately got up from his intense encounter and radical commitment shown by his burning the backup plan and he followed Elisha. You see, Elisha paints a beautiful picture of a concept that I call, "HOLY HUSTLE."

Too many times we are guilty of experiencing God's call, initially responding, and then doing NOTHING. The Scripture doesn't record that Elisha took some time off or waited six months before following Elijah . . . *he followed him immediately!* So many of us have the mindset that, even though we have said "Yes" to God's call, somehow that starts at a later date. It's like we put a "To Be Determined" (T.B.D.) date on our response to God's calling and just slip back into our "normal" life.

> **WE PUT A "TO BE DETERMINED" (T.B.D.) DATE ON OUR RESPONSE TO GOD'S CALLING AND JUST SLIP BACK INTO OUR "NORMAL" LIFE.**
> #THEBURNFACTOR

Elisha started IMMEDIATELY! Listen, God's call on our lives doesn't have a future date of implementation; it starts NOW! Get up and GO! Get your holy hustle on and begin taking steps in the direction of God's divine call! You might not have all of the answers or fully see all of the steps that God has for you, but what is important is that you start moving in that direction!

KEEP MOVING

Too many people have the mindset that God's call starts once they graduate from high school or college or complete that degree or certification or receive a credential. In all reality, God's call starts the moment you hear His voice and say "Yes." Wherever you are, that moment is the time to get started!

Please don't misunderstand what I'm saying. I'm not saying that if you experience a call of God to pastor that you are going to go home and be a Senior Pastor the following Sunday. That is NOT what I'm saying! What I am saying is that when you experience your divine call, it starts when you say "Yes!" In fact, God has been waiting for you to say so, so let's not waste any more time!

In writing his letter to the Church at Rome, Paul notes that he was "called" and "separated" in Romans 1:1. The word that Paul uses for "separated" means "appointed." So Paul was called by God, responded to that call, pursued that call, and then after a season of time was separated or appointed by God to do that particular task. So the call started immediately, but there was a gap of time before he was appointed or serving in that position. What did he do in the meantime? He got his HOLY HUSTLE on. He pursued the call. He kept moving in that direction.

So, in mathematical terms, let's look at it this way. You have this radical God-encounter and experience God's divine call on your life at what we'll refer to as "A." You have a gap in time that we'll call "B," and then you have the end result, "C." So the function would look like this:

A + B = C.

Call + Gap in Time = End Result.

The key to what we experience in the end ("C"), depends on what happens during the gap in time ("B"). This is where so many of us miss it. God is the same yesterday, today, and forever. He's still calling people and confronting lives today just as He did 2,000 years ago. So the "A" moments (or opportunities) for them are still happening every day and that will never change. The reason, however, that we are not experiencing or seeing the desired end results ("C") is because of what's happening in the "B" moments.

God has clearly opened a new door for you to walk through since you have experienced His divine call on your life. Now, don't you dare stop moving! As Jentezen Franklin points out, "When God closes one door, he opens another, but you don't want to hang out very long in the hallway." God has placed His divine call on your life and is moving you into a new area you never dreamed was possible, so whatever it takes, DON'T STOP! START NOW!

You won't be perfect, and you won't always do the right thing, but that is not what is important. What is important is that you keep your eyes on God and His divine call and keep moving in His direction. Follow Him. As Jeannie Mayo says, "God is not interested in PERFECTION, he's far more interested in DIRECTION!" Don't SIT, SLUMBER, or SLOUCH, get moving!

You will make mistakes and sometimes you will do the wrong thing; that is perfectly OK. Losers call it FAILURE; winners call it LEARNING. You are on a journey and you've got your holy hustle on! No time to sit still or give up.

FROM THE BEACH TO THE BOAT

In Mark 6, we read of one of the most incredible miracles in the Bible, Jesus' feeding 5,000 men, not counting women and children. What an amazing experience this must have been to sit on the shores of the Sea of Galilee and watch Jesus take the five loaves and two fish and supernaturally multiply them! After picking up all of the leftovers after this awesome event, Jesus had some very specific instructions for His disciples: "Immediately He made His disciples get into the boat and go before Him to the other side, to Bethsaida, while He sent the multitude away" (Mark 6:45).

Notice that the time came when the followers of Christ had to leave the crowds, get into the boat, and go to the other side. The beach experience was amazing! There was a massive crowd, Jesus was absolutely killing it with His sermon, and then to top it off, He did this incredible miracle! Can you imagine the energy and buzz that was going on?

I've been in some pretty incredible worship services that just left me absolutely stoked out of my mind, but I'm sure they pale in comparison to what it must have felt like there on the shore. No matter how amazing the moment is or was, at some time a transition must take place to move to the next steps in following Christ.

Jesus gave them simple instructions, "Get into the boat and go to the other side." I'm sure it would have been really easy for the disciples to just stay there on the beach. I mean, wow, look what Jesus had just done! And the crowd was still there! There was excitement and energy. It would have been easy to sit and bask in the emotions of the moment, but at some point, the next step had to be taken.

Jesus was on a mission, and He was taking the disciples on a journey. He moved them from the beach to the boat. You see, the boat is where we get our holy hustle on. It's the place that we obey Him. It's where we take the next steps and are shaped and formed into what He's called us to be.

The beach was where the excitement was and the miracles happened, but we can't stay there forever; we are called to follow Him! Jesus was moving on. All too often, many people find themselves hanging around at the beach when they should be moving to the boat to get started carrying out God's divine call for their lives!

CH10: HOLY HUSTLE

This is where most people miss it, because the boat looks too simple. It doesn't seem as awesome as the beach. The beach is where we saw the miracles; the crowd was there, and the excitement and fire was there! But the boat just looks simple. After all, this isn't rocket science; keep this in mind: what were the majority of the disciples? Fishermen. What do fishermen do? They row boats.

You see, Christ is often just waiting to see what we will do. Will we follow His instructions? Even when they seem simple and mundane? Are we really ready to commit and consecrate ourselves to following Him? Or are we more interested in hanging out where all the excitement is?

Sometimes we don't make the transition from our divine encounter to a daily walk of pursuing God's call, all because it seems way too simple. Paul writes to the Church in Corinth in 2 Corinthians 11:3, "But I fear, lest somehow, as the serpent deceived Eve by his craftiness, so your minds may be corrupted from the simplicity that is in Christ."

It's time to get in the boat! I know it sounds simple, but just begin to take steps to follow God and do what He asks you to do! Do what you know to do! You heard His voice calling you out, now simply follow that voice as you recklessly pursue His call on your life.

START! That's it, it can't get any simpler than that! Get into the boat and begin to row.

> *START! THAT'S IT, IT CAN'T GET ANY SIMPLER THAN THAT!*
> #THEBURNFACTOR

You see, this is a process. Think about this, this is the very Son of God. He could have thrown the disciples to the other side. He could have spoken a word and teleported them to the opposite shore, but He didn't. He wanted to see if they were ready to get their holy hustle on.

Wherever you are right now on your journey with Christ, it's time to make a fresh commitment to pursue God's call on your life. A fresh commitment to follow and a fresh commitment to the simplicity of hearing His voice and obeying His commands.

Let's move from the beach to the boat, from the experience to the everyday. Simple leads to supernatural when we are following the voice of the One who called us out of darkness into His marvelous light.

You've got this! As incredible as your God-encounter was, there is another shore to which God is leading you, a place where more miracles will happen, then another and another and another. Don't lose sight of what God called you to do, and don't get lost in the simplicity of following Him daily! And whatever you do, don't you dare put a start date of T.B.D. on God's call on your life.

It starts now!

Just like Elisha, commit to waste no time at all, so get up and get going!

CHAPTER 11

SERVE

"Opportunities are usually disguised as service and hard work. That's why most people never recognize them." —Ann Landers

There is so much to be said today of the almost lost art of servanthood. In a culture that is alarmingly obsessed with self (#selfie), becoming a servant seems to be a passing tradition. Our mindset is often, "Everything revolves around me." Take for example Social ME-dia. We spend countless hours consuming and sharing information that all revolves around ME. What I ate. What shoes I wore today. What I think about my boss. What I think about that new T.V. show.

Me.

Me.

Me.

Me.

We have created a culture in which we not only celebrate and promote ourselves, but we also create heroes out of those who do it even better than us! The cover of the May 20, 2013 issue of *Time* magazine even heralded this generation as the "Me, Me, Me, Generation."[1]

I often wonder what the scene from John 13 would have looked like today. In this passage of Scripture, Jesus and the disciples are getting ready to celebrate Passover, and although the disciples did not know it, this would be there last Passover with Christ. On this particular evening, the Bible records that Jesus and his disciples were having supper together. Now if this were happening in modern times, I believe many of the disciples would have been sending out some pretty sweet posts on social media.

Dinner with Jesus #Blessed.

Chillin' with my boys at the Masters Crib tonight. Don't be #hatin

Peter's fish were legit tonight!

You should have heard Jesus bless the meal #justsayin

Obviously, I'm just having some fun, but don't kid yourself, this tendency to put oneself first and be self-serving is no new concept. In the middle of this meal, Jesus absolutely blows the disciples' minds.

> So he got up from the table, took off his robe, wrapped a towel around his waist, and poured water into a basin. Then he began to wash the disciples' feet, drying them with the towel he had around him. (John 10:4-5, NLT)

Jesus got up and showed by example the very way we are to be living. He washes the disciples' feet as an act of servanthood. Just stop for a moment and think . . . this was one of the last moments on earth that Jesus would have with the disciples. What does He choose to do? He sets an example for them, showing them that this is how they are to live. The disciples are thoroughly confused; here is their Master taking on the form of a slave. Jesus explains,

> I have given you an example to follow. Do as I have done to you. I tell you the truth, slaves are not greater than their master. Nor is the messenger more important than the one who sends the message. Now that you know these things, God will bless you for doing them. (John 10:15-17, NLT)

Jesus knew that it wouldn't be long and this room of influencers and leaders would be going into all the world. He wanted them to have no doubt as to the lives they should live, lives of servanthood. He picked up a towel, humbled himself, and washed their feet.

Elisha understood this concept. He was familiar with being a servant. Think first of all where Elijah finds Elisha. Matthew Henry comments, "He found him, not in the schools of the prophets, but in the field, not reading, nor praying, nor sacrificing, but ploughing."[2] Something is to be said of not only the work ethic, but the servanthood of Elisha.

I love the way author J. Hampton Keathley III, described this concept:

> I think it is also important to note where Elisha was when Elijah found him. Though he belonged to a prominent family, he was at work in the field with the rest of the field hands. Though wealthy, he was not irresponsible or lazy. This didn't make him a leader, but it certainly demonstrated he had already developed the kind of character needed for leadership. Not only did hard work build character, it gave him a testimony to those around him.[3]

So it is apparent that when Elijah finds Elisha, Elisha is familiar with living a lifestyle of servanthood. He's not lazy or self-centered; he is a hard-working servant. Elisha knows how to "DW" or "Do Work." This is why, as the story unfolded that day in the barnyard, the Scriptures record, "Then he arose and followed Elijah, *and became his servant*" (emphasis added). Notice the very first thing that Elisha did: he became Elijah's servant. It is natural for him.

He wastes absolutely no time at all! He experiences his divine call, burns the backup plan, and begins to take the next step in serving. Again, not to rehash what we just covered in the last chapter, but so many people struggle with the transition from their moment of divine calling to living it out every day. They struggle with what to do next.

TAKE NOTE: Elisha gives us the answer: SERVE.

Find the area that you are called to and begin to SERVE. Waste NO TIME. SERVE. The problem is that way too many people love the *concept of serving* much more than they love *actually serving*. On paper, serving looks great!

> **A LOT OF TIMES THE REASON WE DON'T LIKE SERVING IS BECAUSE IT LOOKS TOO MUCH LIKE WORK.**
> #THEBURNFACTOR

A lot of times the reason we don't like serving is because it looks too much like WORK. It's not as much sweet as it is sweat. But it is God's plan that we become servants!

Do you feel like God has given you a divine call to be a foreign missionary? Then until the time comes for that to begin, start serving in that area right now! Pray for missionaries, begin to financially support them. Find anything that has to do with missions and begin serving in that area! As you serve, you are walking out that divine call that God has placed on your life.

Serve.

Serve.

Serve.

It's not complicated. The same can be applied for any type of divine call. Start serving right now! Too many of us sit around waiting for a position, or the right timing or title to come. You already have a title: it is "Servant," so get started!

I love what a pastor friend of mine once said to a room of young leaders, "I started pastoring my current church when I was 13. I served at my dad's church, cleaning toilets and mowing yards. Give 100 percent, wherever you are."

You see, Jesus Himself said in Luke 16:10, "He who is faithful in what is least is faithful also in much." This is a Kingdom principle that must not be overlooked. On the day that Elijah was taken away from Elisha, Elisha had the holy confidence to ask for a double portion of his anointing, because he knew that he had faithfully served his mentor.

DEAD FISH

After graduating from Bible college, I opted to stay an extra year to serve as an intern and to travel with ministry teams at the college.

On one particular day, during our morning chapel prayer service, I got a phone call. Now I know that I shouldn't have looked at my phone during a prayer service, but keep in mind this was back in the day when not everyone had cell phones (like today), and there wasn't a constant barrage of texts, updates, and alerts. I know this is hard to believe, but when your phone went off, it was typically very important, not just an emoticon from your bff, or a snapchat of someone's burrito.

So when my phone began to vibrate that early in the morning, I knew it was important. I looked down to see that our school president's personal assistant was calling me. This was also who I was interning with, so I knew that I should take the call. I ran out into the lobby and answered the phone. I heard this request, "Randy, we need you to come to President Jones' office just as quickly as you can."

I said, "Absolutely," and hung up the phone. I began to run across campus because I just knew deep down inside of my heart that this was going to be absolutely HUGE! I mean getting called to the president's office, and mind you, called out of prayer meeting to go there, surely meant that something big was about to happen!

I just knew that my time had come. The school president was going to ask me to preach, teach, or do something huge. My hard work had paid off and my time had come!

I ran all the way across campus and went directly into his office. As I entered the office, there stood his assistant holding a bag of water with a dead goldfish in it.

I was confused.

"Randy, we have a serious problem, all of President Jones' fish keep dying, and we've got to figure out what's going on with his fish tank. Can you run this dead fish across town to the pet shop and have the water tested?"

At first I didn't know what to say. "Where are the cameras?" I thought to myself . . . surely this is a joke! Then I realized she was serious and I really didn't know what to say! Not because I wasn't willing to go—or didn't want to do it—but because I was trying so hard to not look disappointed!

After a few seconds I said, "Absolutely, no problem at all!"

As I drove across town, I couldn't help but just laugh. Could I have gotten frustrated? Absolutely! My mind and emotions wanted to point out how stupid and silly this was! My thoughts and feeling were pointing out that "someone else" should be doing this! After all, I was too gifted, talented, and anointed to be running over to the pet store for something as minuscule as this! Don't they realize I'm called to preach? Don't they realize I want to change the world? The internal conversation went on and on. But in my spirit, I knew that God was teaching me how to be a servant.

> **THE CONDITION COMES BEFORE THE POSITION.**
> #THEBURNFACTOR

Now years later, I am often reminded by God of that dead fish. He reminds me that if He couldn't trust me to be a servant with a dead fish, then He couldn't trust me with leadership positions of great influence.

Too often we want the title but not the towel. We want the platform but not the plan. We want the mic without the method.

The condition of servanthood comes before any position of influence.

The *condition* comes before the *position*.

Elisha served Elijah.

CH11: SERVE

TEENS IN ACTION

Two of my heroes are my youth pastors, Roger and Wanda Stowers. I owe much to them for the years they loved and invested into my life as an adolescent. One of the things that had a lasting impact on my life was the concept of servanthood that they worked to instill in the students in our youth group.

I'll never forget the day Pastor Wanda got up and announced to our Teen Sunday School class, "We are starting a T.I.A. Program! Teens In Action!" She went on to announce how we were going to begin serving our church on Sunday mornings in a variety of ways. Then she unveiled the new lime-green fluorescent T.I.A. vest that we would be wearing in the parking lot! And we had flashlights! This was like safety patrol on steroids!

Seriously though, I remember how excited we were to get started in this new endeavor. Along with many others, I began showing up early on Sunday mornings to park cars, greet attendees, walk elderly people into the building, and perform other tasks as needed. Whatever was needed, we were there rain or shine!

We were having so much fun, but at the same time, we were learning a very important principle: servanthood. We were learning how important it was to serve. Did we have fun parking cars, directing traffic, and ushering people into the church? Absolutely! But it didn't compare to the joy that we experienced as we learned how to simply serve.

As I grew older, this continued to be instilled in my life. I was already blessed by the fact that I had seen solid examples of the whole servanthood concept in my mother and father. They had portrayed this for me my entire life. After I experienced my spiritual awakening as a teenager and responded to God's call on my life, serving came easy for me due to the foundation they had instilled.

I knew that God called me to ministry, I responded and said "Yes," and then much like Elisha, just simply began to serve. I followed my parents example. Before I ever preached from the pulpit, I vacuumed the sanctuary. Before I ever led a worship chorus, I changed the transparencies. Before I greeted at the front door, I pushed the lawnmower. Before I started a bus route, I cleaned the bus.

I learned how to serve.

SLAVE

Today we often lack the focus on denying oneself and serving others. Serving is not always glitzy or glamorous. It's not always the hip or trendy thing to do, but it is God's process for forming us and shaping us into what He desires us to be: servants.

> **SERVING IS NOT ALWAYS GLITZY OR GLAMOROUS. IT'S NOT ALWAYS THE HIP OR TRENDY THING TO DO, BUT IT IS GOD'S PROCESS.**
> #THEBURNFACTOR

In closing this chapter, think about this. The Greek word for "servant" in the New Testament is *doulos*. It is used over 130 times and the overwhelming majority of the time, it is better translated as "SLAVE." Now that doesn't sound pleasant to our entitled, narcissistic culture, but that is the life that we are called to live.

This is why the Apostle Paul, often started his letters by stating, "This letter is from Paul, a slave of God." *Doulos* literally means "one who gives himself up to another's will."[4] We experience God's divine call, we burn the backup plan, go all in, and start serving another's will, the One whose voice we heard calling us out of darkness into His marvelous light.

In the year 1732, John Leonard Dober and David Nitschman were living common lives in Germany. John was a potter and David was a carpenter. Everything changed for them when they heard that there were 3,000 slaves from Africa who had been recently captured by an

CH11: SERVE

atheistic British slave owner, who transported them to the West Indies to do forced labor in the sugar cane fields.

John and David were not only moved by the atrocity of this act of slavery, but more importantly, by the unthinkable fact that the 3,000 men would be doomed to live and die without ever once hearing the message of the gospel. So after seeking the Lord, they set out to be the first ever Moravian Missionaries.

As they made plans for their trip, they came up against a pretty intense obstacle. They were informed that they would never be allowed in the West Indies as missionaries. The government officials informed them that, "Transport to the Caribbean slave village is not only impossible, but also unthinkable," explaining that only slave owners and slaves were allowed near these Caribbean Islands.

John and David knew that God had called them, and they weren't going to back down. They were ready to go all in, so they did the unthinkable. They sold themselves into slavery and boarded the ships headed to the West Indies. To reach the slaves, they became slaves themselves!

When the ships left the harbor, both men left their families and everything they knew on the shore. In that moment, many of their family and friends continued to call out to the men with great emotion, begging them to change their minds. But as the ship slipped off into the distance, both young men raised their hands toward heaven and declared, "May the Lamb that was slain receive the reward of His suffering!"[5]

Dear friends, we have a divine call on our lives, so let's not give in to the cultural norms that rule our society. Instead, let's follow the example of Christ and become servants!

CHAPTER 12

SUBMIT

"And let them also be tried and investigated and proved first; then, if they turn out to be above reproach, let them serve" —1 Timothy 3:10 (AMP)

As we continue to study the divine pattern for experiencing and responding to God's call, it is imperative to note that Elisha submitted himself to Elijah. He not only became his servant, but he submitted or came under the authority of Elijah. You will see all throughout the Scriptures that God has a divine plan for those who will be taking any role whatsoever in His Kingdom and that role is one of learning to submit.

God is not about the "solo" performers, but rather He is interested in those who are willing to submit themselves to someone else and become accountable and teachable. Once again, we see the process that God lays out to fill the gap of time from the day of experiencing a call to actually walking in that call. That process is learning to submit to someone else's authority.

Elisha is obviously a person of influence already, as noted by the size of his family's farming operation and the size of the oxen team he was using to plow (12 yoke of oxen). But God still had a process that he intended for Elisha to go through; it is the same process He has for you and me as well. This is often where the rubber meets the road, because this is when we learn to set aside our preferences, agendas, and desires and learn to completely submit to someone else's authority.

Would a time come in Elisha's life when he would take a lead role? Absolutely. He would eventually follow right in Elijah's path and actually operate with a double portion of the anointing that was on Elijah's life. In fact, over the span of Elisha's prophetic ministry Scripture records 28 miracles performed by Elisha. How many miracles does Scripture record as being carried out through Elijah? 14! God gave Elisha a double portion![1]

But long before the spiritual spotlight began to shine on Elisha's ministry, he submitted himself to Elijah. So many people miss out on the full capacity of their calling because they aren't willing to submit and come under someone else's authority first.

This is a process.

It is commonly believed that Elisha served Elijah for ten years, staying humbly submitted to his spiritual mentor till the very end. Notice, you don't see him running off, starting his own ministry. You don't see www.elisha.com billboards popping up everywhere in Jerusalem. You don't find Elisha bailing a few years into the process, claiming that Elijah just doesn't have the "mojo" anymore. What do you see? You see Elisha submitted and serving.

Elisha didn't have the reputation of one who was just waiting for his next opportunity or who needed to be in the spotlight; Scripture records that he was known as the one who poured water on the hands of Elijah (Malachi 4:6). He was a humble servant who was submitted to his leader.

THE NEED

The need today for spiritual fathers and mothers who will rise up to mentor the next generation cannot be overstated. Likewise, the same need exists for sons and daughters who are willing to humble themselves and submit to spiritual mentors in their life. These interconnected and interdependent relationships are absolutely vital in this day and age. In our world of rampant independence, this concept looks unappealing to our mind, will, and emotions. But I refuse to believe that submission and mentoring is a lost art. In fact, I believe with all my heart that we can experience a rebirth of the Spirit of Elijah in our culture today, a revival that will turn the hearts of the parents to their children and the children to their parents.

We have enough sermons, stories, resources, and books on mentoring; now we just need to put it into practice! I believe one of the saddest verses in the Bible (*if not the saddest*) is found in Judges 2:10, "When all that generation had been gathered to their fathers, another generation arose after them who did not know the Lord nor the work which He had done for Israel." There is a huge need today to ensure that we are passing on our faith to the next generation.

I always find watching a relay race very interesting. Take for example the 4 × 100 relay race, one in which the United States has historically dominated. Until the 2000 Olympics in Sydney, Australia, the U.S. Women's 4 × 100 Relay Team had won the gold medal from 1984–1996. Total domination! Nothing less was expected of the team in Sydney, because they were hands-down the favorite team. But what happened in Sydney and then repeated again in the '04 and again in the '08 Olympics, left the U.S. Women's team going home with only a Bronze Medal in 2000 and nothing but shattered dreams in the other years.

The problem? A major issue with passing the baton!

The U.S. Women's 4 × 100 Relay Ream had the fastest runners, not only on paper, but on the track as well. However, they failed to successfully pass the baton from one runner to the next. How could something so seemingly small (less than 12 inches long) cause such big problems? The same is true today in our culture when we talk about the simple concept of mentoring. We need each other! We need a rebirth of the Spirit of Elijah in our generation today.

Yes, I understand that mentoring and submission might seem like simple, small and old-fashioned concepts. But if we fail at this process, yes, we might finish the race, but we won't come anywhere close to fulfilling the potential that we have together by using the Father's proven methods.

Just in case you're wondering, at the 2012 Olympics in London, the U.S. Women's 4 × 100 Relay Team nailed their baton exchanges. They not only won the Gold Medal, but finished the race with a time of 40.82, more than a half-second faster than a record that had stood for 27 years.[2]

SPIRITUAL PARENTS

This rebirth first must start in the hearts of spiritual parents who are willing and ready to mentor the next generation. Paul, in writing to the Church at Corinth, stated, "For though you might have ten thousand instructors in Christ, yet you do not have many fathers." The same is true today. There is a great need for those like Elijah who are willing to turn their hearts to the next generation and invest their lives into others.

We have many great preachers, teachers, pastors, prophets, and the list could go on and on . . . but we are genuinely lacking fathers and mothers! I'm sure you've heard it said about mentoring the next generation, "They don't need a sage on the stage, but a guide by their side." There is so much truth to this in being a mentor to others; those you are mentoring want to know that you are there *with* them.

As a kid playing ball, I always knew when Dad was in the stands. He didn't have to say anything at all during the game (however this is nearly impossible, because he's a competitive person). All he had to do was just be there; in my mind, it made all the difference in the world! Today as I experience the joy of being a father, my absolute favorite part of watching my children play sports happens as I catch them peeking out of the corners of their eyes to see if I'm watching. I love this! They just want to know I'm there!

Anna Stoehr, 114, was the oldest living person in Minnesota, until her passing in December 2014. In the fall of 2014, she befriended Verizon sales representative Joseph Ramireza, who sold an iPhone to her 85-year-old son. Anna had decided at her young age (#yolo) to setup a Facebook account. So, with the help of her new friend, Anna set out to join the world of Facebook.

Upon trying to get started, Anna encountered a roadblock. She discovered that Facebook doesn't let you choose a date of birth before 1905, and Stoehr was born in 1900. So she did what many people do on the Internet, and lied about her age, choosing 99.

Stoehr, with a little help from her new friend Joseph Ramireza, decided to write a letter to Mark Zuckerberg, founder of Facebook. Stoehr's message was simple, yet profound. She got out her typewriter and eloquently stated: "I'm still here."[3]

> *A GENERATION OF SPIRITUAL SONS AND DAUGHTERS ARE JUST LONGING TO KNOW THAT YOU ARE STILL HERE!*
> #THEBURNFACTOR

More than anything, today a generation of spiritual sons and daughters are just longing to know that you are still here! They need you in their lives!

SPIRITUAL SONS AND DAUGHTERS

On the flip side of the coin, we must have an awakening of the sons and daughters that will cause them to turn to the parents. As noted earlier in this chapter, this concept of submitting to others flies in the face of today's cultural norms. In a culture that celebrates 15 minutes of fame, more than a lifetime of faithfulness, submission, and service just doesn't seem popular. However, we need the spiritual covering that is provided by the Elijahs in our lives. Without it, we will not be able to live up to our full potential!

There is not only a new level of productivity that comes from submitting, but also a new level of supernatural protection. They (mentors) have something we need. God is watching you, "Elisha," to see how you will respond to the "Elijah" He has placed in your life.

Several years ago, officials at the Kruger National Park and Game Reserve in South Africa were faced with a problem. Their growing population of once-endangered African elephants had grown beyond what the park could sustain. A plan was crafted to move some of the elephants to other game reserves. The elephants were to be air-lifted in special harnesses and carried by helicopters to the other reserves.

> **GOD IS WATCHING YOU, "ELISHA," TO SEE HOW YOU WILL RESPOND TO THE "ELIJAH" HE HAS PLACED IN YOUR LIFE.**
> #THEBURNFACTOR

Another problem arose when it was discovered that the harnesses couldn't carry the massive adult African bull elephants. Quickly searching for a solution, it was determined to leave the adult male elephants in the main reserve and only transport some of the female and juvenile males.

The crisis was solved. However, as time passed a new problem arose at Pilanesburg National Park, the new game reserve where the younger elephants had been relocated. Park Rangers at this South African game preserve began finding dead bodies of the endangered White Rhinoceros.

At first they thought this was the work of poachers; however, the rhinos had not died from gunshots, but had apparently been violently killed by deep puncture wounds. The rangers set up cameras throughout the park to try to solve the mystery. What they discovered was unbelievable.

The culprits were the aggressive juvenile male elephants that had been relocated to the park just a few years earlier. The young males were seen on camera chasing down the rhinos, knocking them over and beating them to death with their tusks. Not only that, but it was discovered that these young males were terrorizing other animals in the park as well. This behavior was alarming as well as extremely rare.

The rangers settled on a theory. The only thing missing from the relocated herd was the large dominant bull elephants. In the wild, it was these adult male elephants that modeled right behavior and set an example for the younger elephants. To test their theory, they created stronger harnesses and relocated some of the adult male elephants from Kruger to the park. Within a very short time, the problems were solved and the erratic, violent behavior stopped.

The younger elephants began to change as they followed the example of the adult elephants who modeled what it was like to be an elephant.[4]

Regardless of the stage of life we are in, we need mentors who can provide the spiritual influence we need. They often see what we can't see, and they've been were we've never been! Yes, I know we have a burning fire inside us to go and change the world and be mightily used by God! Who placed that calling there? God, the same Person who called Elisha and placed him in submission UNDER Elijah.

Submit yourself to the spiritual influence that God has placed in your life. At the right time, you will find yourself with more fruit and favor then you could ever have imagined. Why? Because you didn't go about it on your own! In the words of Christine Caine, "If He assigned you, then He'll find you! Stay where He placed you!"

UNDER/OVER

I'm convinced that one of the last great awakenings will come as God pours out His Spirit on all flesh, helping us to rediscover the power of "Under/Over." Under/Over is the posture we are to have as leaders.

We should have someone that we are submitted to (under) and we should have someone that we are mentoring over (Under/Over). It is simple, but not easy. If we can find this correct relational balance in our lives, we will be well on our way to making a profound impact in the world in which we live.

It starts by submitting.

Elisha submitted to Elijah and became his servant.

The choice is ours, so let's choose to swim against the cultural tide of isolation and independence and learn the freedom and joy found in submitting to one another in the fear of God.

SECTION 5

DIVINE FOCUS

CHAPTER 13
STRAIGHT AHEAD

"Consecrate, then concentrate." —Dwight L. Moody

"Look straight ahead, and fix your eyes on what lies before you"
—Proverbs 4:25, NLT

In a world where we are bombarded with distractions, the art of focusing seems to be almost lost. If you've ever downloaded an app on your cellular device or tablet, the first question the app will ask is, "May I send you notifications?"

Let me translate that for you: "I would like to be added to the thousands of other things pulling for your attention during the day." If you haven't already figured this out, the answer for this question is always, "NO!" With the growth of technology, the pressure to do more in less time and to be everywhere at once, we have almost forgotten what it means to truly focus on something.

Everywhere we go, something or someone is vying for our attention. Companies actually spend millions of dollars a year to come up with ways to try to do just that, catch our attention. The chaos just grows and grows.

One of my favorite Disney movies is *Up*. I must confess, although this is no big shocker for those who know me, I cried the first time I watched this movie; I thought it had an incredible story-line. One of my favorite characters in the movie is Dug, the dog.

Dug can speak English via a special collar that translates thoughts into speech. In the movie, Dug says some funny stuff for sure, but hands-down my favorite part is when Dug is in the middle of a sentence, gets completely distracted and yells, "Squirrel!"

Why do I love this scene so much? It's because I can relate! I have many "Squirrel Moments" in my daily journey. It takes no effort at all in our world today to become distracted. We must relearn the art of focusing.

When Elisha is coming to the end of his time with Elijah in 2 Kings 2, we notice an intense focus that exists in Elisha's mind, heart, and actions. His mind is set on one thing: staying with Elisha.

> And it came to pass, when the Lord was about to take up Elijah into heaven by a whirlwind, that Elijah went with Elisha from Gilgal. Then Elijah said to Elisha, "Stay here, please, for the Lord has sent me on to Bethel." But Elisha said, "As the Lord lives, and as your soul lives, I will not leave you!"

Stop and think about this: Elisha realizes the power of the moment in which he is living. He knows that his master is about to be taken away. The mantle is getting ready to be handed down to him. In essence, everything Elisha has consecrated and prepared himself for until this moment is getting ready to happen. This is why Elisha is FOCUSED!

Elisha's supernatural barnyard experience with God's call is years behind him now. The goosebumps from the spiritual high of burning the plowing equipment and going all in are gone. Elisha has been serving under Elijah now for many years, but he still demonstrates the same intense spiritual focus that he had in the past as he tells Elijah, "I will not leave you!"

Too often we miss spiritual breaking points in our lives because we allow the enemy to distract us from the divine moment that we are living in! What would have happened if Elisha would have been distracted in this holy moment? Maybe it would have been like this: "That's fine, Elijah, you go on ahead to Gilgal, I'm gonna sit over here and check out my Instagram feed and see what the other prophets have been up to recently." Or maybe it would have been: "Yeah, go ahead, Elijah, I'll meet you in Gilgal. I'm just about to break my high score in Candy Crush, I'll catch you in a little while."

Elisha was focused. He was in the moment and was not about to let anything keep him from getting his double portion. He had given up too much, served too hard, and prayed too many prayers to get distracted now. He was focused!

CAPTIVATED

You can always tell when someone is really focused on something because it becomes their number one priority. In that moment, they have the ability to make everything else disappear and focus on only one thing.

For me, most of the time, I'm able to multitask very well. However, if you turn on a West Virginia Mountaineers football game, I can only do one thing: watch the game. I can't have a conversation, read, write, or anything else . . . unless you count eating and yelling at the TV. Don't get me wrong, I might talk, but my focus is on one thing: the game! I've also learned over the years that if someone should try to have a conversation with me during those games, I'm not responsible, nor should I be held liable for anything I commit to or say yes to in those conversations!

The bottom line is that we have the ability to focus on one thing and push aside distractions when something has captivated our hearts and minds! For some of us, this comes more naturally than others, but by God's grace we can all learn to focus and prioritize!

Let me give you an example. My number one strength is competition.

I hate to lose and love to win. I'm not mean about it; I just wanna kick your butt at whatever game we're playing, period. So when something has captivated my attention (like a competition), I'm naturally more inclined to focus on the goal, which would be winning.

This became evident to me as I played trumpet in my middle school band. In that band, you were seated or ranked in your particular instrumental section based on how you performed your scales. A few times a year, we were tested on our scales and those with the quickest times without mistakes were given the top seats. These scales were played on our own time and recorded on cassette tapes (I know many of you will have to Google it) and handed in to the teacher. In essence, we could do as many takes or tries as it took to get our absolute best times down.

I still vividly remember sitting in my bedroom as a sixth grade student staring at my trumpet and my old-school tape recorder. "I've got you this time," I would say to myself before I pressed "Record" and tried to play those scales as quickly as I could. I would literally work for hours trying to lay down the fastest track ever! I was unbelievably focused!

With great pride I announce to you that I was a first-seat trumpet player for Pulaski Middle School for my entire three years! Why? Because I was focused! I was captivated by the thought of being the best. I couldn't even imagine what it would feel like to have to give up that first chair, so each time I worked harder and harder.

> **IF CHRIST CAPTIVATES YOUR HEART DAILY, THEN STAYING FOCUSED ON YOUR CALLING WILL HAPPEN NATURALLY.**
> #THEBURNFACTOR

Our calling should captivate us. Yes, we know that it is captivating when we first experience it, like Elisha in the barnyard, but what about years later? What about further along in the process, when you feel like your time is never going to come?

CH13: STRAIGHT AHEAD

You may feel like you've missed it, because everyone else seems to be getting noticed, doors are opening for everyone else but you. All your friends seem to be getting used by God, and here you are, stuck in someone else's shadow.

Stay focused, Elisha! Your season is just around the corner! Don't miss it, stay in the moment!

In the end it's a heart that is completely captivated by Christ that allows us to stay focused on our calling. If Christ captivates your heart daily, then staying focused on your calling will happen naturally.

THE HOLY HONDA

When I was 21, I did something completely out of character. One day, out of the blue, I decided that I wanted a motorcycle. I had never driven a motorcycle ever before, nor had I really expressed interest in one, but out of nowhere, I got the fever bad! I was too young to be experiencing a midlife crisis, yet I wasn't sure what was going on in the inside of me. I was only sure of one thing: I wanted a motorcycle! The open road was calling my name.

At the time I was single, had a decent job, and could afford one, so I bought a brand new Honda Shadow Aero 750. She was a sight! I was psyched out of my mind to get this thing home! After we transported the bike home, the time finally came for me to ride it for the first time. Keep in my mind, I had never ridden a motorcycle before of any size, much less one this large. All that I knew about riding a motorcycle was the book knowledge I needed to pass my learner's exam.

I still remember standing in front of the bike as it was sitting in my parent's driveway, just "a-shining." My friend Mike rolled up on his motorcycle, ready to take me out for my first lesson. Most of our family had gathered around for the big occasion. I was just about to fire up my bike for its inaugural ride, when my Dad came out the front door.

I noticed that he had an intense look on his face that told me he was on a mission. He was also carrying a bottle in his hand, and it wasn't a bottle of water for my ride, it was a bottle of anointing oil. He quickly announced, "All right, everyone gather around, I'm not about to let you venture out on this thing without me first praying over it!"

At that moment, my Dad didn't care how silly it may have seemed or how messy he was about to get my bike with the oil. He was focused on only one thing: declaring God's divine protection over his son as he set out on his new ride. Others may have thought it was old-fashioned, but He didn't care; he was focused. He proceeded to anoint my bike and to call down angels over every mile that my Honda Shadow would ever traverse. He was focused!

There comes a time in our lives when we almost have to "flip a switch" in our spirits. That's when we take it up a notch, regardless of how silly we may look or feel, and really focus on the task that is before us! I remember coming home from our Youth Conference that summer and flipping that switch in my life. One of the first things I did was to take a black permanent marker and use it to write "STAY FOCUSED" in big bold letters on the wall beside my bed. (Disclaimer: I got my parent's permission first!) As a result, every day I would see this reminder and determine not to be pulled off course.

> **ELISHA REALIZED HE COULDN'T AFFORD TO BECOME LAZY IN HIS PURSUIT; HE COULDN'T AFFORD TO BECOME DISTRACTED.**
> #THEBURNFACTOR

We have to learn how to push past all the distractions that pull us to the right or to the left and make us miss our holy moment! There is a lot at stake here! Elisha realized he couldn't afford to become lazy in his pursuit; he couldn't afford to become distracted.

You have a divine call on your life! Stay focused!

THE POWER OF FOCUS

Henrietta Cornelia Mears was born in Fargo, North Dakota, on October 23, 1890, the youngest of seven children. She grew up in a good Christian home in which her parents laid a strong spiritual foundation for her life.

At the age of 7, on Easter Sunday morning, Henrietta gave her life to Christ and declared her faith in Christ. By 17, Henrietta responded to a challenge from her pastor, Dr. Riley, and made a public commitment to vocational Christian service. At that time she felt in her heart that she was called to be a missionary to China. She would later discover that her calling was to train and equip others to take the gospel throughout the world.

At 20, Henrietta experienced a painful loss with the passing of her mother, who had a profound impact on her life. Her pastor, Dr. Riley, mentioned the passing of the "spiritual mantle" from her mother to her during the memorial service. Pondering this thought brought about an intense focus in Henrietta's life that caused her to fully surrender her life to Christ.

From the time when she experienced her call at 17, up to that very moment, Henrietta had remained faithful to serving God in every open door. She taught Bible classes while in college, went on to teach, directed public schools, and faithfully served in her church. She had a profound impact in the local communities in which she lived. Now her focus became even more intense.

In the fall of 1928, Henrietta felt God calling her to Hollywood, California, as she accepted the position of Director of Christian Education at First Presbyterian Church. Under her leadership, this Sunday School grew from 450 to over 6,000 by 1933! It later grew to 6,500, becoming the largest Presbyterian Sunday School in the world.

She held this position for 35 years and left her imprint on a countless number of lives. Her direct influence has been noted on such Christian leaders as Billy Graham, Bill Bright (founder of Campus Crusade for Christ), and Jim Rayburn (founder of Young Life), to name a few. It would be nearly impossible to measure her indirect influence on the body of Christ around the world, but it is unmistakably significant. Think about this: Campus Crusade alone has impacted hundreds of thousands of college students and the world at large, through various mission outreaches, including the *Jesus Film*, which by the year 2000, had been seen by over 4.5 billion people. One writer in *Christianity Today* called Henrietta "the grandmother of us all."[1]

Take note of the fact that Henrietta experienced and said yes to her calling at 17. It wasn't until 21 years later that she found herself as a Christian Education Director in Hollywood, California. It was during those 21 years Henrietta focused on completely surrendering her life to Christ and devoted herself to His calling on her life. Her focus and consecration to God's call prepared her to bear much fruit.

What is it you need to focus on right now?

What things are you allowing to pull your attention away from God?

What is keeping you from fully focusing on Him in this moment in which He has placed you?

Allow the Holy Spirit to re-align your focus! You've come too far in this process to lose sight of the next level that God has for you. Focus!

CHAPTER 14

THE POWER OF "NO"

"I will not leave you!" —Elisha

My wife and I are absolutely blessed with our four children. Raising them is hands-down the most exciting thing that I get to be a part of. It is amazing to me how each one of them are so alike, yet uniquely different. One common characteristic that all four of our children have is that they come preprogrammed to say the word, "No!" I am not sure how this happened, but I believe it is just a standard feature with all children, straight from the factory.

"No" is a powerful word and it doesn't always have to have a negative connotation. There are many moments in life when it is not only healthy, but absolutely imperative that we learn how, when, and where to say "No."

In the closing moments of the Elijah and Elisha journey, an interesting dialogue transpires between the two. As I pointed out in the last chapter, Elijah asks Elisha to stay in Gilgal as he travels on to Bethel. Elisha refuses to stay and basically says, "No, I will not leave you, Elijah." Elijah goes on to offer the same suggestion to Elisha, not one more time, but two more times, asking him to stay while he goes on to Jericho and then to the Jordan River.

You see, Elisha stays focused on the moment and sticks with his answer of, "No I'm not leaving you." Elijah wasn't wanting some "alone time" here; he didn't have some important meeting that he needed to attend . . . well, he sort of had a ride coming for him, but that's a different story! Elijah was simply testing Elisha to see if he was really focused and ready for the next step in the process.

Many of us miss out on our next level in God or in service to His divine calling simply because we lack the discernment of when to say "No" to some things and remain focused on the task at hand.

Often we think of this concept of saying "No" as only pertaining to all the "bad things" in life.

Say no to sin.

Say no to temptation.

Say no to the Devil.

That is all factual information. However, often what keeps us from moving to the next level or season of growth is our inability to say no to things that aren't necessarily bad; they just aren't the right things!

> **IT IS IMPERATIVE WE LEARN THAT A GOOD THING AT THE WRONG TIME IS A BAD THING.**
> #THEBURNFACTOR

It is imperative we learn that a good thing at the wrong time is a bad thing. Good often becomes an enemy of the best! It wouldn't necessarily have been a bad thing for Elisha to honor Elijah's request to "stay put" at Gilgal, would it? After all, the second time he asked, they were in Bethel and surrounded by the school of the prophets. For crying out loud, Elisha could have stayed and had a rompin,' stompin,' good ol' time with his prophet friends! Please understand that would not have been a bad thing, it was just the wrong thing, because it was NOT what

Elisha was to be doing in the moment.

We have to learn the power of saying "No!"

CHOICES

Immediately upon my return home from my God-encounter at the Elisha Generation Youth Conference, I knew that I had to make some monumental choices. I wasn't engaged in any gross sin or any detrimental relationships, but I knew that I had said "Yes" to God's call and I had to make a shift in my focus.

There were some things that were good in my life, but if they were to remain, they would keep me from really focusing on what I knew God was calling me to do. I knew I had to learn to say "No".

One very specific area was high school athletics. I had been rigorously training for eight months with a personal trainer, had lost over sixty pounds and was making full preparations to play football in the coming fall. I knew well the hard work and dedication that I had put in over the past few months to prepare myself to compete. I also knew deep down inside what I had experienced was real, and I knew that God was calling me to focus and dive in with all my heart.

I had to make a decision to say "No" to my childhood dream of playing football and focus 100 percent on God's call. Now, please don't misunderstand me! I'm NOT saying a person can't play sports in high school, college, or at any level and still pursue God's calling on his or her life. I'm not saying that at all. What I *am* saying is that I knew in the season in which God had placed me, that I must intensify my focus and remove distraction. I knew I wasn't going to go on and attempt to play ball at the next level, so while playing my junior and senior years would have been fun, it would have taken up hours of my life that I needed to focus in the areas God was calling me to.

It was one of the most important decisions that I've ever made in my life. It was a defining moment for me, because by saying "No" to what I originally thought was a good thing, I was saying "Yes" to a God thing and focusing 100 percent on pursuing His call.

Unfortunately, not everyone shared my excitement. The individual who had been training me for months didn't understand, and to say the least, was very upset with my decision. He was a believer but yet didn't understand my seemingly rash decision.

And then came the fun part, informing my high school Head Football Coach of my decision. I still remember the exact place I was standing that day on our athletic track having just finished a jog, when I informed him. After telling him of my decision, he looked in the eyes of this 15-year-old kid and said my problem was that I was weak, a big pansy, and would never amount to anything in life.

This was all a part of my testing.

God wanted to see if I really did want to focus on what He had for me to discover. You see, there comes a moment when we have to make some choices. When you make those choices, be prepared for the fact that not everyone will see eye-to-eye with you, and that is perfectly OK! It doesn't make them bad people; more importantly, it doesn't make you any better than they. Just stay focused and determined to pursue what God has called you to do.

As I continued my journey, I realized that there were many other things God would ask of me, things that maybe not everyone else would understand. There were some things I felt He asked me to do that not even my "Christian" friends understood. I would later come to understand that on our journey, there are some things that won't disqualify us from the race, but they will slow us down! The writer of Hebrews exhorted us,

> . . . let us lay aside every weight, and the sin which so easily ensnares us, and let us run with endurance the race that is set before us. (Hebrews 12:1)

Yes, we understand we need to say "No" to sin, but often we need

CH14: THE POWER OF "NO"

to learn to say "No" to the unnecessary weights that slow us down. The things you're saying "No" to won't necessarily send you to Hell, but they aren't helping you on the journey to which God has called you.

Remember, good is often enemy of the best.

SILENCING THE VOICES

Not only did Elisha have to convince Elijah (three times!) that he was not going to leave him, he also had to silence some negative voices around him.

> Now the sons of the prophets who were at Bethel came out to Elisha, and said to him, "Do you know that the LORD will take away your master from over you today?"
> And he said, "Yes, I know; keep silent!" (2 Kings 2:3)

It is imperative that we learn from Elisha's example; understand that there are going to be some influential voices in your life that you will have to learn to silence. Elisha was in the moment at a crucial point of his journey. He wasn't about to let someone's negative comments distract him!

If there is anything that can cause us to lose focus, it's when we get caught up listening to friends who like to run their mouths! If you stop and listen, they will talk you *out of* what God has called you *in to*!

You've got to learn to silence the voices!

The apostle Paul wrote to the Church at Galatia, asking them a simple question,

"You ran well. *WHO* hindered you from obeying the truth?" (Galatians 5:7, emphasis added). Notice he asked them specifically "who," not what! I've heard it said if God wants to bless you, He will send a person, and if Satan wants to curse you, he will send a person. You've got

> *YOU'VE GOT TO LEARN TO SILENCE THE VOICES!*
> #THEBURNFACTOR

to learn to position yourself with the right people who have the right perspective.

I'm reminded of a story I heard about twin boys. Although they were twins, they had completely different personalities. One was a total pessimist, and the other an optimist. Their personalities became so extreme that their parents decided to take them to see a psychiatrist.

The psychiatrist took the young boy who was an extreme pessimist and placed him in a room piled to the ceiling with brand-new toys. Upon entering the boy immediately burst into tears. "What's the matter?" the psychiatrist asked, extremely confused. "Wouldn't you like to play with any of these new toys?" "Yes," the young boy cried, "but if I did, I'd only break them!"

Next the psychiatrist took the extreme optimist into a room piled to the ceiling with horse manure, thinking for sure this would dampen his outlook. Quite the opposite happened! As he entered the room, the boy let out a loud yelp of joy, a response that the psychiatrist had hoped to get out of his brother in the room full of new toys. The young man quickly scurried to the top of the manure pile, dropped to his knees and began gleefully digging. Completely baffled, the psychiatrist asked, "What in the world are you doing?" The young boy replied, "With all this manure, there must be a pony in here somewhere!"

> YOU DON'T HAVE TIME TO GET CAUGHT UP IN THE NEGATIVE AGENDAS OF OTHERS.
> #THEBURNFACTOR

I absolutely love that story! It has significance for you and me. We must learn to surround ourselves with people who can find the ponies! We must silence the voices of those who want to pull us aside and distract us from our journey. You don't have time to get caught up in the negative agendas of others; stay focused on your calling and destiny!

NO FEAR

Some other things that we have to learn to say "No" to in this process are fear and intimidation. In Gilgal and Bethel, on both occasions, the prophets said to Elisha, "Do you know that the Lord will take away your master from over you today?" You can sense the intimidation in their voices. They were essentially tormenting or harassing Elisha with the thought that Elijah was about to be taken away from him.

Scripture records that 50 of the prophets followed Elijah and Elisha all the way to the Jordan River, watching from a distance. Elisha had to learn how to press on through the fear and intimidation that he was surely feeling in these moments.

This is often easier said than done. Fear and intimidation are things that we all face, and the Enemy loves to use them to keep us from pursuing God's divine calling on our lives. What is interesting is that there are over 2,000 fears or phobias that have been identified in the human experience. However, according to psychologists, human beings are born with just two basic fears: the fear of loud noises and the fear of falling.[1] All other fears are learned!

I was baffled by this great number of phobias, so I decided to look them up. Here are a few of my favorites:

Coulrophobia—fear of clowns (not restricted to evil clowns).
Coprostasophobia—fear of constipation.
Dentophobia, odontophobia—fear of dentists and dental procedures.
Emetophobia—fear of vomiting.
Halitophobia—fear of bad breath.
Nomophobia—fear of being out of mobile phone contact.
Papaphobia—fear of the Pope.

Turophobia—fear of cheese.

Phobophobia—fear of having a phobia or of fear.[2]

The enemy loves to bring fear to keep us from reaching our full potential! In the final moments right before Elisha is about to receive a double portion of Elijah's anointing, what does the enemy use? Fear and intimidation!

The enemy would love nothing more than to keep you bound up in fear and cause you to lose your focus!

Eng and Chang Bunker were born on May 11, 1811, in the fishing village of Meklong, Siam (today called Thailand). They were conjoined twins and became an absolute spectacle for everyone who encountered them. People from all over the world were filled with curiosity about their condition. Many doctors came to study them. Today we refer to conjoined twins as "Siamese Twins;" the name comes from Eng and Chang from Siam.

At age 17, they began touring the world as a sight-seeing attraction. They drew large crowds of curious onlookers wherever they went. In 1832, the twins moved to the United States and began touring with P.T. Barnum, making a pretty good living for themselves.

In 1839 they quit the traveling exhibition life and settled down in Wilkesboro, North Carolina, where they became farmers. In the same year they became United States citizens and were given the official name "Eng and Chang Bunker." Their surname, Bunker, was adopted from the name of a bystander, Fred Bunker.

In 1843 Chang and Eng met two sisters, Adelaide and Sarah Ann Yates, whom they married. Chang married Adelaide and Eng married Sarah Ann. They had two separate homes where they would alternate three days at one home and then three days at the next home. Between the two families, they had 21 children!

After the Civil War (which took a hard financial toll on the Bunker families), the twins returned to the exhibition life, but they were not as

CH14: THE POWER OF "NO"

successful as before. Around this time, the twins started inquiring as to whether an operation could successfully separate them.

In 1871 Chang suffered a stroke, and although he recovered, his health started to deteriorate. In January of 1874 Chang contracted bronchitis, and died in his sleep. Doctors were frantically summoned to try to separate the them, but within two hours Eng died as well. It was determined that Chang died of a cerebral blood clot and Eng literally died of sheer terror.[3]

Fear claimed Eng's life!

Fear is a powerful force. What kind of fear is the Enemy using to distract you from completely focusing on God's divine call on your life? Is it a fear of the unknown, a fear of being misunderstood, the fear of rejection, or even the fear of failure?

These are all legitimate concerns that each of us have faced; however, if we are to experience the greater things God has for our life, including a double portion of His Spirit, we have to learn to push past these fears!

When God called Moses to lead the Children of Israel out of Egypt into the Promised Land, Moses insisted that God had chosen the wrong person!

> Lord, I'm not very good with words. I never have been,
> and I'm not now, even though you have spoken to me.
> I get tongue-tied, and my words get tangled. (Exodus
> 4:10, NLT)

Moses is saying that since he can't speak, he shouldn't be the leader. However, it is interesting to note that the book of Acts records of Moses that he was, "taught all the wisdom of the Egyptians, and he was powerful in both speech and action" (7:22, NLT).

Somewhere along the way fear had gripped Moses' heart and had convinced him he couldn't do it. What is holding you back from taking the next step? It's time to silence the voices of fear and intimidation in our lives to radically pursue what God has called us to do!

CHAPTER 15

HUNGRY FOR MORE

And so it was, when they had crossed over, that Elijah said to Elisha, "Ask! What may I do for you, before I am taken away from you?" Elisha said, "Please let a double portion of your spirit be upon me." —2 Kings 2:9

Elisha had faithfully served Elijah for many years. He had been faithful to respond to God's call, completely surrendered all, and been fully committed throughout the entire process. Now in this intense moment, Elisha knows Elijah is about to be taken away from him, and the story comes to an apex with a question posed by Elijah.

It wasn't anything fancy, just a simple question. "What may I do for you?"

In this moment, we get a brief picture into the intense hunger that Elisha still has to serve God and his call. Elisha lays everything on the table. He goes all out. Should we expect anything less from the barnyard bonfire man? He asked Elijah for a double portion of his spirit to rest upon him. Double!

Without hesitation, Elisha asked for double! He wants more. He wants God to use him in twice the magnitude that He used Elijah.

Twice the miracles.

Twice the number of changed lives.

Twice the impact.

He asked for a double portion.

Elisha went for it. This was his moment and nothing was going to hold him back from going for it. Nothing!

A CRAZY CRAVING

Have you ever had a deep craving for something? Like to the point where you would just about do anything to satisfy that craving?

Not long ago, I was privileged to travel with a team of friends to Brazil for a missions trip. During a portion of the trip, our ministry team traveled many hours up the Amazon River to some very remote villages. Traveling up the Amazon River on a boat and sleeping in hammocks was an absolutely amazing experience I will never forget!

After a few days of ministry, our team was slated to depart and return down the Amazon River. After finishing the last day of ministry, which included some pretty demanding physical labor in the hot tropical climate, a nice cold soda sounded great to many of our team members.

Nightfall set in and everyone was on board the boat. As the crew was making preparations to set sail, someone decided to make a last-minute run back to the village. The plan was to drop off some food with the village pastor, and more importantly (I know that sounds terrible), buy some cold soda from the makeshift village market. Taking the food to the pastor was basically our excuse to get the soda, but, hey, it had been a long week!

> *IT IS IMPERATIVE WE LEARN THAT A GOOD THING AT THE WRONG TIME IS A BAD THING.*
>
> #THEBURNFACTOR

Neither my best friend, Joe, nor I, had any idea about this plan for soda; all we knew was that the people going back to the village needed some help, so we volunteered to hop on the little johnboat with one of our Brazilian friends and a crew member.

CH15: HUNGRY FOR MORE

As the four of us headed to the village, we happened to notice that the large boat (our ride home) was moving away from shore! We thought to ourselves, "Well, surely this won't take long and we'll catch them before they get too far." We quickly made our way up into the village and delivered the food and stopped by the makeshift market where the soda deal was going down. The problem, however, was that this took a little longer than expected. By the time we got back to where our boat had been, it had sailed out of sight!

I was getting just a little concerned now. We hopped in the johnboat and the young crew member who was driving seemed to be a little nervous himself. He opened up the throttle all the way as we took off. The problem, however, is that the village was in a pretty narrow and tight tributary that had to be carefully traversed to get back out to the main part of the Amazon. This young man, however, had one thing on his mind, and that was catching the big boat!

Since I was sitting up front, I watched as not once, not twice, but three times we nearly ran aground and sent our boat flipping over into the murky Amazon. Mind you, before the impromptu soda run, our group had been spotting alligators from the big boat!

We were lost, it was dark, the driver couldn't figure out the channel, and we couldn't speak a lick of Portuguese! Joe and I just looked at each other and kind of laughed, because neither of us wanted to admit to the other we were scared!

Finally, we found our way out onto the river, eventually catching up to the big boat! A crowd gathered on the lower deck as we came aboard. Everyone was asking, "What took you guys so long?"

My heart was still pounding from the adventure, so all I could say was, "I sure hope you guys enjoy your SODA!"

We've gotten many laughs and good memories from that dark night on the Amazon. You better believe we both had our fair share of the soda that night!

You see, when you crave something, you go after it with everything that you have. You relentlessly pursue it and refuse to slow down or give up. While others may fade, fall, and get fatigued, you stay fixed and focused on the goal.

It doesn't matter how long you've been on the journey, the hunger and passion is still inside you. You are willing to do whatever it takes to get more of the Lord's power in your life. The psalmist said it this way, "As the deer longs for streams of water, so I long for you, O God" (Psalm 42:10, NLT). It is an intense craving that refuses to let you get pulled aside, distracted, or intimidated. It pushes you forward and gives you the holy tenacity to ask for a double portion!

LITMUS TEST

As children, we come out of the womb hungry. Babies will instinctively let you know when they are hungry because they come with a built-in appetite! Anytime any of our four children would cry, my solution was always simple: "Let's feed them."

Easy solution, for me, at least!

It is no different in our spiritual life. When we are first saved, we taste and see that the Lord is good, and a spiritual appetite is ignited inside us! When you first experience Christ and the beauty of salvation, you start out hungry!

No one has to push you to worship.

No one has to push you to read the Word.

No one has to push you to pray.

Something comes alive inside you and you are hungry! As Peter said, " . . . as newborn babes, desire the pure milk of the word, that you may grow thereby" (1 Peter 2:2). You are radically changed and you are hungry!

In a real sense, the litmus test for the health of your spiritual life is your appetite.

Think about this: if you're not eating or have lost your appetite, more than likely something is wrong. What is one of the first questions doctors ask, "Have you lost your appetite?" An appetite or hunger is also a sign of spiritual health. It proves that we are alive on the inside and growing! The fire is not dead and we are hungry for more!

> *IN A REAL SENSE, THE LITMUS TEST FOR THE HEALTH OF YOUR SPIRITUAL LIFE IS YOUR APPETITE.*
> #THEBURNFACTOR

I truly experienced this returning home after my life was absolutely transformed by God at the youth conference. I remember how hungry and passionate I was to know more of the Lord. I was so determined to not let the fire burn out!

I learned that true spiritual hunger will cause you to create new priorities and new habits. My spiritual life became a priority for me. Previously, it had just been a *part* of my life, now it *was* my life! I determined to have a quiet time with God every day, something I had never done before in my life.

I remember taking all of my favorite worship songs and dumping them onto a cassette tape. I would play this tape of worship music, and it would help me learn how to focus in on God in worship and prayer. My bedroom was transformed into a Bible college as I learned how to seek God on my own for the first time in my life!

A few weeks passed and it was time to go back to school. I was so determined not to fall back into my old routines. I wanted to keep my quiet time with God as the starting part of my day. I was starting my junior year and also entering a new program at school which required me to be there 90 minutes before everyone else. I could sense the pressure building, but I was determined not to let my hunger fade!

Faithfully, I would set my alarm every morning at a time that I previously thought only existed one time a day (in the PM!) and get up and have my quiet time with the Lord. Yes, I know you can have your quiet time with God any time of the day, but for me, I knew that it must be the first thing at the start of the day. I quickly learned that if I didn't *prepare* for the day, I would soon have to *repair* the day.

It's funny, even to this day years later, I can remember the focused intensity I had for those moments. I was hungry! I didn't want to miss that time for anything! God was revealing Himself to me. On one occasion, I remember saying goodnight to my family and heading to bed. After sleeping, my alarm went off (or at least in my head it did), and like any other morning, I dragged my tired self out of bed and headed to the shower.

> *I QUICKLY LEARNED THAT IF I DIDN'T PREPARE FOR THE DAY, I WOULD SOON HAVE TO REPAIR THE DAY.*
> #THEBURNFACTOR

Next, I returned to my room and began to seek after the Lord, like every other morning. A few minutes later my Mom knocked on the door, came in and asked, "Did I just hear the shower? What are you doing?" She looked confused, which caused me to be confused, so I explained, "I'm just doing my devotions and getting ready for the day like normal, Momma." She laughed and said, "Son, it's 11:30 PM, go back to bed!"

I was so determined not to miss those moments because they were the lifeline of my spiritual life! I was hungry to know Jesus more, and this caused me to shift my priorities and habits.

SPIRITUAL APATHY

As I look back on those early years of my spiritual awakening when God did so much shaping and forming in my life, I'm often challenged to ensure that I'm still pursuing God with that same spiritual fervency. You see, it's easy to lose that hunger and drive. So, I continually keep this before me to make sure that my heart is truly seeking after God.

The truth is that it's all too easy to fall into a satisfied mode, a way of living in which we don't even realize that we are slowly losing our spiritual appetite. Much like the church at Ephesus, everything might look good on the outside, but internally we have left our first love!

It's amazing how some people feel that we should at some point, "Move on," from those early experiences as we "mature" into some pseudo-religious lifestyle in which everything becomes routine. Friend, I don't know about you, but I don't want to ever lose the fire! May I never get to the point where spiritual apathy becomes the normal operating procedure for my life!

I want to be like Elisha, in pursuit of more of the Lord! There is a double portion on the table for the taking, and it's just waiting for anyone who wants it! Don't allow your spiritual appetite to diminish! Don't become satisfied with the mundane, average, everyday, dry, religious routine.

Immediately after Elijah was taken to heaven and Elisha picked up his mantle, an interesting conversation happens between Elisha and the men of Jericho. The men of Jericho come to the newly anointed Elisha and say, "Please notice, the situation of this city is pleasant, as my lord sees; but the water is bad, and the ground barren" (2 Kings 2:19).

This at first seems like a paradox. How can the city be "pleasant" when the water is bad and the ground is barren? How can one person, much less the men or leaders of the city, ever describe a situation like this as "pleasant?"

How could that be?

The answer is that they had become spiritually apathetic.

When we lose our hunger and thirst for more of the Lord, we slowly become comfortable and content with our depraved situation. It becomes our new "normal." I see a similarity between what the men of Jericho said to Elisha and what I hear from many believers and churches today. Everything is pleasant in their eyes, even though the water is bad and the ground is barren. There is no fresh move of the Holy Spirit and no spiritual or numerical fruit can be seen. They are seemingly one step away from spiritual death and decay, but yet things are "pleasant."

Once when I was doing some research on appetite, I came across this information from an article entitled "The Journey towards Death":

> The dying person may experience reduced appetite and weight loss as the body begins to slow down. The body doesn't need the energy from food that it once did. The dying person may be sleeping more now and not engaging in activities they once enjoyed. They no longer need the nourishment from food they once did. The body does a wonderful thing during this time as altered body chemistry produces a mild sense of euphoria. They are neither hungry nor thirsty and are not suffering in any way by not eating. It is an expected part of the journey they have begun.[1]

This mild sense of euphoria is where we find many in the Church today! Don't allow yourself to fall into this trap because it is the beginning of the end for you spiritually! Stay hungry! Like Elisha, continue the pursuit of what God has called you to do!

BURIED ALIVE

In the 18th and 19th centuries, a legitimate fear existed of being buried alive. This fear was heightened during the cholera epidemics. To avoid the spread of this infectious disease, there was a frequent need to expedite burials. This was coupled with the fact that the medical profession often lacked equipment and expertise to properly distinguish between death and near-death states. With this concern growing, many "safety caskets" were developed.

CH15: HUNGRY FOR MORE

In 1829, Dr. Johann Gottfried Taberger designed such a safety casket in which a system of strings would be attached to the corpse that traversed up a tube to a bell at the top of the casket. A casing surrounding the bell kept it from being accidentally rung and prevented rainwater from entering the tube. In the event that a person would be buried alive, his or body movement would cause the bell to ring, alerting the cemetery watchman that someone was alive. The watchman would then insert a second tube down the pipe and pump air into the coffin to keep the individual alive until the casket could be dug up.[2]

The sound of the bell set off an alarm saying, "I know you thought I was dead, but I'm not; I'm still alive!" Some of you reading this might feel like you're dying on the inside. Perhaps you know you've lost your spiritual appetite, and it's not what it used to be. I'm telling you, there is still something inside you that can be awakened!

The Psalmist said, "In my distress I called upon the Lord, And cried out to my God; He heard my voice" (Psalm 18:6). You've come too far to give up now! Let a cry rise from deep inside your spirit to God! Ask him to re-create that holy hunger in you! He's listening and ready: He is not hard of hearing, nor does He lack the ability to respond to your cry.

Refuse to go out silently and slip into spiritual apathy! Cry out to God and allow Him to revive your spiritual appetite!

CHAPTER 16

GO FOR IT!

"We have a culture that will not be changed by the mildly interested."
—Jeanne Mayo

I would love to know what was running through Elisha's mind during those few moments after Elijah was taken up into Heaven in the chariot of fire. As he sat on the banks of the Jordan River with Elijah's mantle in his hand, I'm sure there were many things going through his mind.

I'm sure he thought of the day Elijah encountered him in the barnyard.

I would think he smiled to himself as he thought of the looks on everyone's faces when he slaughtered the oxen and burned the plowing equipment.

I'm sure he shed some tears as he thought of all the mighty miracles he had witnessed through the hands of Elijah.

And then at some point, he looked down in his hands at that precious mantle. It all started to make sense. He could sense the Holy presence of God coming upon him, much like the day he was blindsided by God's divine call. He knew the fire of God was burning inside him.

Now was his time!

CONCLUSION

He had said "Yes!" He had consecrated his life, burning the backup plan in complete surrender. He had faithfully served these many years, submitted to the ministry of his spiritual mentor. Although much time had passed, he was as focused and hungry that day as he was on the day he met Elijah and started his journey.

It was his time to go for it!

> Then he took the mantle of Elijah that had fallen from him, and struck the water, and said, "Where is the LORD God of Elijah?" And when he also had struck the water, it was divided this way and that; and Elisha crossed over. (2 Kings 2:14)

Minutes after Elijah was gone, we witness Elisha's first miracle. It was a repeat of the same miracle that Elijah had just performed on the opposite side of the Jordan when they both crossed over. This is the first of a long line of miracles that would soon be carried out over Elisha's lifetime. But what would have happened if Elisha just sat there?

Elisha wasn't content just to sit on the bank of the Jordan with his double portion anointing. He was ready to go and change the world. He did it by going for it!

Keep in mind there was no guarantee how the situation would play out when he struck the water; not only this, he had an audience of onlookers. But this didn't seem to faze Elisha because he was ready to go!

Are you ready to make a difference in this world? The world is waiting for modern day Elishas who will give

> **THE WORLD IS WAITING FOR MODERN DAY ELISHAS WHO WILL GIVE EVERYTHING TO THE CALL OF GOD, PICK UP THE MANTLE AND GO!**
> #THEBURNFACTOR

everything to the call of God, pick up the mantle and go! Countless lives await the impact of a generation of young and old who will rise up and pursue God's call on their lives.

Unashamed and unapologetic, they have something that is missing in our world today: they have the Burn Factor.

Now is your time.

The mantle is in your hand.

The world is waiting . . .

ENDNOTES

CHAPTER 2

1. Merriam-Webster.com, s.v. "Alter." http://www.merriam-webster.com/dictionary/alter (accessed February 18, 2015).

CHAPTER 3

1. Wikipedia, s.v. "Impact Bias." http://en.wikipedia.org/wiki/Impact_bias (accessed February 18, 2015).

CHAPTER 4

1. James Clash, *Forbes to the Limits: Pushing Yourself to the Edge in Adventure and in Business* (Hoboken: John Wiley & Sons, Inc., 2003).

2. Bruce Lowitt "Bannister Stuns World with 4-Minute Mile," *St. Petersburg Times* (December 17, 1999).

CHAPTER 5

1. Jon Warner, "Making Great Decisions," in *Ready to Manage*. http://blog.readytomanage.com/making-great-decisions/ (accessed February 20, 2015).

2. Maryland DNR, "Deer Facts," DNR Maryland.gov. http://dnr.maryland.gov/wildlife/Hunt_Trap/deer/wtdeerfacts.asp (accessed February 20, 2015).

3. Clairborne Ray, "The Twilight Zone," *The New York Times* (November 29, 2010).

CHAPTER 6

1. NASA, "July 20, 1969: One Giant Leap for Mankind." NASA.gov. http://www.nasa.gov/mission_pages/apollo/apollo11.html#.VOXMLnZrn-Y (accessed February 20, 2015).

2. David Guzik, "The Study Guide for Joshua 10," *Blue Letter Bible*. http://www.blueletterbible.org/Comm/guzik_david/StudyGuide_Jos/Jos_10.cfm?a=197009 (accessed February 20, 2015).

3. Caleb Colley, *The Omnipotence of God* (Montgomery: Apologetics Press, 2004).

ENDNOTES

CHAPTER 7

1. Caleb Wygal, "Transcript of Bill Stewart's Leave No Doubt Speech," WVU PROS. http://wvupros.com/featured/transcript-bill-stewarts-leave-doubt-speech/ (accessed February 21, 2015).

2. Michael Walker, "WVU Football: Where Does the Expression 'Leave No Doubt' Come From?" *Bleacher Report.* http://bleacherreport.com/articles/1295919-wvu-football-expression-leave-no-doubt-where-does-that-come-from (accessed February 21, 2015).

CHAPTER 8

1. Mark Batterson, *All In* (Grand Rapids: Zondervan, 2013).

2. Jessie Szalay, "Hernan Cortes: Coqueror of the Aztecs," *Live Science.* http://www.livescience.com/39238-hernan-cortes-conqueror-of-the-aztecs.html (accessed February 23, 2015).

CHAPTER 9

1. Sudip Khadka, Interviewed by Randy Lawrence, Personal Interview, Email (April 2, 2015). For more information please visit: www.compassionforasia.org.

2. Billy Graham Center Archives, "Jim Elliot Quote," Wheaton College. http://www2.wheaton.edu/bgc/archives/faq/20.htm (accessed February 24, 2015).

3. *Christianity*, "Jim Elliot: No Fool," Christianity.com. http://www.christianity.com/church/church-history/church-history-for-kids/jim-elliot-no-fool-11634862.html (accessed February 24, 2015).

4. William Farley, "D.L. Moody and 19th-Century Mass Evangelism," *Enrichment Journal*. http://enrichmentjournal.ag.org/200702/200702_128_Moody.cfm (accessed February 24, 2015).

5. Paul Chappell, "What God Can Do with a Surrendered Life," *Daily in the Word*. http://www.dailyintheword.org/rooted/what-god-can-do-with-a-surrendered-life (accessed February 25, 2015).

CHAPTER 11

1. Joel Stein, "The Me Me Me Generation," *Time Magazine* (May 20, 2013).

2. Matthew Henry, "Commentary on 1 Kings 19," *Blue Letter Bible*. http://www.blueletterbible.org/Comm/mhc/1Ki/1Ki_019.cfm?a=310019 (accessed February 27, 2015).

3. J. Hampton Keathley III, "Studies in the Life of Elijah," Bible.org. https://bible.org/seriespage/17-taking-your-mantle-1-kings-1919-21 (accessed February 27, 2015).

4. *Bible Study Tools*, "Doulos," Biblestudy.com. http://www.biblestudytools.com/lexicons/greek/nas/doulos.html (accessed February 27, 2015).

5. Tom Zawacki, "John Leonard Dober and David Nitschman," *Emancipation of the Freed*. http://emancipationofthefreed.blogspot.com/2007/01/john-leonard-dober-and-david-nitschman.html (accessed February 25, 2015).

CHAPTER 12

1. David Pyles, "A Double Portion of Thy Spirit." http://www.bcbsr.com/survey/eli.html (accessed February 24, 2015).

2. Associated Press, "U.S. Smashes Women's 4 × 100 Mark," ESPN. http://espn.go.com/olympics/summer/2012/trackandfield/story/_/id/8256748/2012-london-olympics-us-shatters-women-4x100-relay-world-record (accessed February 24, 2015).

3. Dana Thiede, "Facebook's Oldest Fan Dies at 114," *USA TODAY* (December 24, 2014). http://www.usatoday.com/story/news/nation/2014/12/23/facebook-centenarian-dies/20837393/(accessed February 27, 2015).

4. Sam Becker, "Of Elephants and Men," Sports Leader Blog, August 31, 2012. http://www.sportsleader.org/2012/08/of-elephants-and-men (accessed February 27, 2015).

CHAPTER 13

1. Richard Leyda, "Protestant Educators: Henrietta Mears," *Talbot School of Theology*. http://www.talbot.edu/ce20/educators/protestant/henrietta_mears/ (accessed February 27, 2015).

CHAPTER 14

1. Donald Dossey, "A Phobia Primer," *Fears, Phobias and Stress*. http://www.drdossey.com/phobias.html (accessed February 25, 2015).

2. *Oxford Dictionaries*, "List of Phobias." http://www.oxforddictionaries.com/us/words/phobias-list (accessed February 26, 2015).

3. *North Carolina History Project*, "Eng and Chang Bunker (1811—1874)." http://www.northcarolinahistory.org/encyclopedia/395/entry (accessed February 27, 2015).

ENDNOTES

CHAPTER 15

1. Angela Morrow, "The Journey towards Death," *About Health*. http://dying.about.com/od/thedyingprocess/a/process.htm (accessed February 27, 2015).

2. Christopher Dibble, "The Dead Ringer: Medicine, Poe, and the Fear of Premature Burial." http://www.medicinae.org/e16 (accessed February 25, 2015).

ACKNOWLEDGEMENTS

When everything is said and done, I want those who know me the best, to love me the most. My family means the world to me. To my wife Dawn, I am grateful for the gift that God gave me in you. You are my rock. Your love for God and our family is inspiring. To my kiddos, Chase, Maia, Cali, and Jaxon, you bring unspeakable joy to my life, and you always provide me with plenty of wonderful stories to write about! May you increase in wisdom, knowledge, in the favor of God and man. This is our journey together.

To my parents, thank you for a lifetime of faithfulness, I am who I am today because of you.

Thank you to Bishop Charles G. Scott, for your support and encouragment on this project.

Thank you to all those I've had the privilege of working with over the past eight years at the PCG International Offices. Your love for God is inspiring and I'm grateful for your impact on my life.

Thank you to Brian Ramos for your insight and work on this project.

Finally, thank you to the many Elijah's I've had in my life (you know who you are). You have pushed me to run faster, dig deeper, and never give up in pursuit of our high calling. I'm grateful for you.

ABOUT THE AUTHOR

Randy has a tremendous passion to serve his generation. He has served the body of Christ in a variety of leadership roles with global influence. He currently serves as the National Youth Director for the PCG, which leads over half a million Churches worldwide. He is a sought-after communicator and has devoted his life to recklessly pursuing God's call to reach this generation.

He holds a MA in Leadership and Management from Liberty University. Randy and his wife, Dawn, and their four children, Chase, Maia, Cali, and Jaxon reside in Fort Worth, Texas.

@RANDALLKENTJR

FOR MORE INFORMATION

RANDY LAWRENCE

THE BURN FACTOR
ALL FOR THE CALL

For more information on this book and other resources please visit:

WWW.RANDYLAWRENCEJR.COM